Remembering Britten

By the same author

Opera on Record (*editor*)
Wagner's Ring: An Introduction

Alan Blyth

Remembering Britten

Hutchinson
London Melbourne Sydney Auckland Johannesburg

Hutchinson & Co. (Publishers) Ltd

An imprint of the Hutchinson Publishing Group

3 Fitzroy Square, London W1P 6JD

Hutchinson Group (Australia) Pty Ltd
30-32 Cremorne Street, Richmond South, Victoria 3121
PO Box 151, Broadway, New South Wales 2007

Hutchinson Group (NZ) Ltd
32-34 View Road, PO Box 40-086, Glenfield, Auckland 10

Hutchinson Group (SA) (Pty) Ltd
PO Box 337, Bergvlei 2012, South Africa

First published 1981

Set in Linoterm Baskerville
by Book Economy Services, Cuckfield, Sussex

Printed in Great Britain by the Anchor Press Ltd
and bound by Wm Brendon & Son Ltd, both of Tiptree, Essex

British Library Cataloguing in Publication Data
Remembering Britten.
1. Britten, Benjamin
2. Composers – England – Biography
I. Blyth, Alan
780′.92′4 ML410.B853

ISBN 0 09 144950 2

Contents

Illustrations

Benjamin Britten and Colin Graham at a rehearsal for the English Opera Group production of Britten's realization of *The Beggar's Opera*. (*Reg Wilson*)

Recording Britten's second Parable for Church Performance, *The Burning Fiery Furnace*. (*Richard Adeney*)

Britten in the garden of The Red House, Aldeburgh. (*Decca*)

Benjamin Britten with William Servaes during Britten's last visit to Venice. (*Rita Thomson*)

Benjamin Britten and Peter Pears in the garden with Murray Perahia. (*Rita Thomson*)

Donald Mitchell talking to Britten at a garden party. (*Nigel Luckhurst*)

Britten discussing the score of *Phaedra* with Steuart Bedford. (*Nigel Luckhurst*)

Britten with Dame Janet Baker and Colin Matthews. (*Nigel Luckhurst*)

Preface
Alan Blyth

All of those brought up in the musical world of the past fifty years owe a considerable debt to Benjamin Britten. He, almost single-handedly, freed British music from what often seemed to be the stultifying effects of his predecessors, who were rooted all too firmly in either a conservative or a parochial idiom. With his early song cycles, and even more startlingly with *Peter Grimes,* he showed us a new world of sound, yet one that was in no way too revolutionary a break with the past. His music had the qualities he looked for in other composers' music – magic and efficiency (see Sir Peter Pears's comments). He had an almost uncanny facility in writing music – that quality which brought the cry of 'cleverness' from jealous contemporaries in his early years – but he also had the magic, genius, call it what you will, that clothed the 'efficiency' in meaning and feeling.

He also had magic as a man – 'charm' is perhaps the word most frequently used by those who knew and worked with him. Like most great men, he also had a darker side; as you will read, he could be tetchy, peremptory, ruthless, but he usually showed that dark side with good reason – to a colleague or friend whom he felt might not be serving the cause of music as whole-heartedly as he ought.

My purpose in collecting the memories of those who knew the composer best is to preserve the first-hand accounts of how a great composer lived, worked and behaved. Not surprisingly, there are contradictions in these pages. As Janet Baker comments, 'We show different sides to different people,' and it seems this was particularly true of Britten. However, I think that by the end a fair and comprehensive picture of the composer emerges from the views of his friends and colleagues.

I have tried to choose people who knew him at different periods of his life, but inevitably and rightly there is a good deal of overlapping. Some names that one might expect to see included are absent – either because they are unwilling at present to express their opinions, or because I felt they would only duplicate what others had already said. I have not sought to impose a uniform pattern on each contribution, but allowed each chapter take its own shape. I thought it would be of interest to include two examples of Britten's own writing, both of which first appeared in *Opera* magazine.

This book is not intended to be a biography. That immense task is being undertaken by Donald Mitchell, who has been kind enough to be a contributor here and also offered his help.

I would like to thank two people in particular for their advice: Joan Cross, for encouraging me to persevere with what I considered a somewhat daunting task, and Basil Coleman. Also, Merion Bowen for his assistance on Sir Michael Tippett's material; the executors of the Britten Estate for all extracts from his unpublished letters; and to the editor of the *Musical Times* for extracts from Imogen Holst's article 'Working for Benjamin Britten' (1977). As on other occasions, Kevin McDermott at Hutchinson has been a patient and thoughtful editor.

Ben said to me on more than one occasion that criticism should not be one's whole life. I hope he would have appreciated how I have taken his sensible words to heart in the preparation of this volume.

Benjamin Britten
on Verdi and *Peter Grimes*

Verdi[1]

Several years ago I had the occasion to hear a series of performances of those two old favourites, *Traviata* and *Bohème*. At the time my feelings towards Verdi and Puccini were about the same – both of them efficient, with routine and apt stage-craft, but not very interesting musically. So I was not surprised when after four or five performances I never wanted to hear *Bohème* again. In spite of its neatness, I became sickened by the cheapness and emptiness of the music. On the other hand, I was surprised to find myself looking forward with excitement to each successive performance of *Traviata*. In fact, after at least a dozen performances I felt I was only just beginning to know it, to appreciate its depths of emotion and musical strength. That was the beginning of a devotion to the music of Verdi which grows greater as I grow older, as I get to know fresh works of his, and deepen my understanding of the ones I already know.

To analyse a devotion to an art is beyond me, but here are a few observations, which I hope will explain a little why I love the music of Verdi so much.

The variety and strength of his melodies. Verdi can, of course, write the obvious square tunes, which use many repetitions of the same little phrase and work to an effective climax. These abound in the earlier operas, and are immediately endearing: I think particularly of 'Parigi, o cara' in *Traviata*. But he can also write the long casual lines, a succession of apparently unrelated phrases, which repeated hearings discover to have an

[1] From a symposium first published in *Opera*, Vol. II, No. 3 (February 1951).

enormous tension deep below the surface. The wonderful 'conversational' duet at the end of Act I of *Otello* is a case in point.

The perpetual 'unobviousness' of his harmonies. Verdi has the gift, which only the greatest have had: that of writing a succession of the simplest harmonies in such a way as to sound surprising and yet 'right'. The accompaniment to the Egyptian trumpet tune in *Aida* is an extreme example of this. Then later in his life he developed a new kind of harmonic originality, which I can most easily describe by reminding the reader of the astounding string accompaniment to the bell strokes in the last scene of *Falstaff*, and the obscure *Ave Maria* 'on an enigmatic scale' from the *Quattro Pezzi Sacri*.

His attitude to the voices on the stage and the orchestra. This seems to me to be perfectly right. The voices dominate, and the orchestra is the background – but what a background! In the later works especially, the orchestra has a range of colours wider than with any other composer. For soft shadings, the Nile scene in *Aida* is inimitable, and no one has ever made the orchestra roar so terrifyingly as at the beginning of *Otello*.

In the construction of his later works Verdi seems to have discovered the secret of perfection. At the beginning of his life he accepted the convention of the times in the sharp definition of the numbers, and he balanced these numbers brilliantly. Fundamentally, he never changed this attitude, but later on the numbers melt into each other with a really astonishing subtlety. The fact that the most famous composer alive today dismisses *Otello* and *Falstaff* 'because they are not written in numbers' shows, it seems to me, that he does not know the works very well.

And so on. I have no space to write about his vitality, his breadth of humanity, his courage, his extraordinary career which developed into an almost divine serenity. I should like to end with a personal confession. I am an arrogant and impatient listener; but in the case of a few composers, a very few, when I hear a work I do not like I am convinced it is my own fault. Verdi is one of these composers.

Peter Grimes[2]

I have been present at only three foreign productions of *Peter Grimes* (the two in Switzerland and the American premiere at Tanglewood) and I have heard, in addition, perhaps three or four more broadcast. The fact is that I believe in writing new operas and not in following the old ones around – there is not time for both. But I have had, of course, detailed reports from friends who have been at many other performances, and so I have formed some idea of how the work fares when away from home.

The conclusion I have come to is that *Peter Grimes* makes the greater impression in the more modest performances – without perhaps great stars – provided that it is thoroughly rehearsed, intelligently presented (visually and aurally) with the energies devoted to the general picture rather than the detail. The singers must, of course, have good voices, but these should be used to interpret the music and not for self-glorification. I suspect that this applies to all other operas ever written but I only assert it categorically here, since I wrote this particular one!

Travelling in Canada, I have had this conclusion confirmed, when hearing a recording of a CBC broadcast of *Peter Grimes* in Toronto. It was given by what, I gather, is developing into a permanent company formed for broadcasting operas. Few of the singers are known outside Canada and most of them have a hard time earning their living there by singing. This opera company is not commercially sponsored, but performs in the so-called 'Wednesday Nights' – evenings kept free for longer and more serious 'cultural' entertainments, which obviously would not interest advertisers. All the same, the audiences for these evenings are very big (which shows how silly advertisers can be); and this production of *Grimes* attracted so many listeners and made such an impression that the air was 'cleared' the following week and the whole programme repeated.

[2]Discussion of a broadcast, first published in *Opera*, Vol. I, No. 2 (April 1950).

The performance itself made its impact largely through an extremely simple and intelligent production. The diction and characterisation of the singers were excellent (never at the expense of the line) so that the events were always clear. This clarity was also helped by intelligent positioning in front of the microphone (I think it is called 'aural perspective') rather than by elaborate commentary. Let me say, without more delay, that the producer was a young man who recently emigrated from England, where he was associated with Decca records – Terence Gibbs. It is fair to say that he was the driving force behind the whole undertaking.

No production, however good, could have been so effective had not the musical side been really well thought out, carefully rehearsed and executed with unusual talent. I was told that the preparation of the work took a whole year. Now, it is all very well having a long time to rehearse and plan but you must have ideas and the ability to communicate them. Any conductor can rush through a three-hour rehearsal and then dash off a concert in the evening: give most of them several long rehearsals and they are lost. The ability of this conductor, Geoffrey Waddington, came as a complete surprise to me: he was first-rate. The orchestra, of good quality, played with great precision and accuracy, and the ensemble singing was also of a high order. Above all, my composer's heart was warmed by the fact that he used the right tempi. In the whole work, there were only perhaps three tempi which he misjudged and that shows he knew the speeds at which the music was singable and playable, and the speeds at which the passages 'sound' and make sense. How grateful I was for that! The singers' devotion to the task in hand was memorable and most moving. There were perhaps not any fantastic voices in the cast but they could all of them sing. Some of the secondary parts I have never heard better done – Boles or Mrs Sedley, for instance. Frances James (Ellen Orford) was perhaps the best-known singer in the cast: she is obviously intelligent and gifted, and she made a most sympathetic character. The Peter Grimes of William Morton was quite remarkable. This young singer has a voice of just the right timbre. It was not too heavy, which makes the character simply a sadist, nor was it too lyric, which makes it a boring opera about a sentimental poet *manqué*; but it had, as it should, the elements of both.

What do we learn from this extraordinary performance, which induced acute homesickness in the breasts of two Aldeburghians 4000 miles from home? One learns I think that to make sense of an opera we should examine it closely – its notes and words, and the hints given as to production in the stage directions – and forget preconceived theories. If the work has overtones or undercurrents, let them appear by themselves and do not emphasise them; that is sure to put the work out of joint. Having found what is actually in a piece, let us perform it with skill, energy, discipline and humility. In defiance of many high-brows today, who have developed a kind of inverted snobbery about singing, let it be understood that to have a gigantic or a creamily beautiful voice is not enough – one must know how to sing. If Rossini really did say that about '*voce, voce e più voce*', he was following the example of so many critics (both of the journalist and 'dining-out' variety) in saying the apt or witty remark rather than the true one.

1
Sir Peter Pears

As Britten's companion for the best part of forty years, Peter Pears played a crucial part in the composer's life of music. Not only did Britten write most of the major tenor roles in his operas for Pears, beginning with Peter Grimes and culminating in Aschenbach, but the two also shared the platforms in recitals that remain cherished memories to those who heard them. Both their friendship and their professional work together began in the late 1930s. Although they first met in 1934, when Pears was a member of the BBC Singers, they did not begin their life together until three years later, after the death of Pears's close friend, Peter Burra, in an air accident.

As Sir Peter recalls, they gave their first recital together in 1937, at Cambridge in aid of Spanish Civil War Relief. During their period in the United States, when they were giving recitals in aid of wartime charities, they quickly established a pattern that was to change little over the years (except, of course, when they were giving one of the Schubert or Schumann cycles). First there would be a group of early English songs – usually Dowland and/or Purcell – followed by a Schubert group, and finally some of Britten's own work and folksong arrangements.

The premiere of one of Britten's cycles – the *Michelangelo Sonnets* – was given at the Wigmore Hall in the autumn of 1942 and marked Britten's and Pears's return to Britain. The success of this event caused Walter Legge of EMI to ask the pair to record the work; this was the first recording they made together. Although at this distance of time that occasion may seem to have marked a significant advance in the composer's reputation, Sir Peter is at pains to emphasize that it then seemed part of a steady development. Britten was anxious only to write fruitfully for specific events and for specific people: 'He was always moving towards the next goal. At this juncture it was *Peter Grimes*. When the opera appeared, the reception was overwhelmingly favourable and the success undoubtedly heartened Ben. There were a few unfavourable reviews, but he was never put off by adversely critical remarks if he felt the public had responded to what he had tried to achieve.'

It was the same in his work as an executant. He had a clear vision of how the music in hand should sound, and he adhered to his ideas. As a creative artist himself, he was able to respond sympathetically to the inspiration of others.

The relationship between Pears and Britten at recitals was naturally closer than that of many other pairs. Each instinctively responded to the other. 'Ben was extraordinarily sensitive as a pianist, both to what I wanted to do with a song and in what he wanted to achieve. He could make lighter sounds than anyone else I can recall; he was anxious to imitate the timbre of early pianos rather than emphasizing that of a modern Steinway. In the Schubert cycles he knew precisely what colour he wanted to project, and he managed to do it because of the speed with which his brain could communicate with the tips of his fingers. That was an extraordinary phenomenon: mind and hands seemed in constant touch and, although he was aware of the need to practise, there seemed to be no question of technique coming between his thoughts and their execution.

'At the same time he was capable of playing immaculately the most difficult pieces – his own concerto, for instance, or Liszt's *Gnomenreigen*. He had his own method of fingering, which other, more regular, players might find strange, but he worked out his own ideas very carefully. What he wanted to achieve had to come naturally to him.'

Britten was undoubtedly nervous before a recital, particularly in his later years, when he could 'freeze' before appearing on the platform. He thought that this affected his playing in the first few songs of any programme but, as he warmed to his task, he forgot his qualms. On the other hand, he remained at all times responsive to his partner's state of voice.

In his conducting, as in his playing, music came before technique. His inexperience in the early days showed in the strain he suffered in his shoulder, particularly when he had to take over the premiere of *Billy Budd* from an indisposed Josef Krips. As the years went by, he overcame such difficulties. His accomplishments in conducting were admired by many orchestras – most of all by the players of the English Chamber Orchestra. 'They appreciated the fact that he loved to make music with them. His rehearsing was always to the point; he hated to waste a moment. I think, in that respect, he learnt much from Frank [Bridge]. He detested inattention. If players weren't following him, as sometimes happened with larger orchestras, he could be sharp in his reactions. He deplored inefficiency in any professional musician, but he wasn't inhuman towards frailty. Above all, he needed people to be attentive.'

If Britten was not composing or playing or conducting, he was concerned with the organization of the Aldeburgh Festival. 'He wasn't an administrator by nature, but together we managed to plan – by ourselves – the early festivals. As the years went by, we were joined by other artistic directors, who brought with them new ideas, but the reins remained firmly in our hands. We naturally tended to plan programmes around the artists who were available and what they might like to perform.'

Yet hours spent on other activities were hours taken away from writing. 'And Ben did consider it his first task to compose. For that reason he kept to a regular schedule at home. He began work at eight-thirty or nine o'clock and continued without interruption until a late lunch about one-fifteen. After lunch he used to go for a long walk during which he often worked out ideas. He resumed composing at about five o'clock and went on until dinner at eight o'clock. Even if he seemed to have a composing block, he remained at his desk getting on with some other kind of practical job.

'At the end of the day he liked to try out on the piano what he had managed to write during the course of it. I would be consulted about the vocal line if the piece in hand was a work written for me. We also discussed the texts in the first place. Ben needed to find a poem or even a line that suggested a musical idea before he would alight on it for setting. On occasion, he would begin a song and not complete it. Others he completed but never published because they didn't fit into any cycle.'

He was not dogmatic over the interpretation of his own work. 'He understood that there might be an interpretation other than his own. In his own performances he had a very positive attitude. He knew what he wanted. If an artist missed the point of a piece or some part of it, he was irritated. In a similar way, he regarded the original productions of all his stage works as definitive and often disliked their successors. For instance, he didn't like the second, Covent Garden, production of *Peter Grimes*, by Tony [Tyrone] Guthrie with designs by Tanya Moiseiwitsch, because three-quarters of the set comprised a representation of the sea. Guthrie, something of a bully, forced the composer to accept it. Ben and I had imagined the sea as being in the orchestra so it was not necessary to see it on stage. The first production was more sensible, less pretentious: you could sense the enclosing, claustrophobic feeling of the Borough. By contrast, Ben was perfectly prepared to accept new productions, such as Colin Graham's *Gloriana*, when they seemed to be faithful to the original.'

In the case of particular roles, he viewed some re-interpretations unfavourably. He always felt that a singer's personality had to be right for his part. That was why he was so careful in his own casting and was dubious about some choices in houses or productions over which he had no control. In general, he was chary of big voices – the important thing was that the voice had to express character.

Britten had definite attitudes towards composers of the past. Take Brahms: he admitted to having a passion for Brahms in his youth, but later he fell out of love with him. 'Ben seems to have reacted strongly against the sound world of Brahms. He found it too thick and unimaginative. He had more ambivalent feelings towards Beethoven. While he may have been critical of parts of Beethoven's orchestration – indeed attempted to guy them in the last act of *A Midsummer Night's Dream* – he continued to respect him as much as he had in younger days. He couldn't help but be aware of the beauty in much of Beethoven's music.'

He loved Mozart and Schubert without qualification. He admired Bach, Dowland and Purcell, as well as the madrigalists – in his youth he had sung madrigals with a group conducted by Arnold Foster. Although he had a poor view of his own voice, he liked to sing, just as he liked to play the viola in chamber music with local quartets. 'When we were in America, we used to call at the local library for works for viola and piano. I used to play the piano part.'

Britten appreciated Mahler (though he could be critical of him), and admired Tchaikovsky, particularly for his orchestration, and Debussy and Ravel for the same reason. 'I always urged Ben to write a book on orchestration, because of what he said about the work of these composers and because he considered the existing studies on the subject to be inadequate. But that was never to be.'

He had pronounced views on some of his contemporaries. He admired Stravinsky's early ballet scores and the *Symphony of Psalms*, but he felt that Paris had lent Stravinsky's work a chic air, which had been encouraged by Nadia Boulanger, who seemed to think that this period in his work was outstanding. Although Britten considered this later writing of Stravinsky mannered, he acknowledged his extraordinary ear. 'Ben wanted to hear most of all in other composer's music magic and efficiency. The magic cannot be explained; the efficiency is something any good composer should have.'

He was immediately impressed by Shostakovich when he heard the first symphony in the 1930s, and never wavered in his admiration for his Russian colleague. 'He liked the clear, unfussy directness of Shostakovich's music and its vitality. Their friendship was deep and genuine. Ben was able to get past the "edgy shell" to the true man.'

In their relationships with other contemporaries, Britten and Pears often found their friends to be those with whom they were working at any particular time. 'If, after that, we weren't in collaboration for a while, we might not find time to see them. I don't think that friendships were broken when for some reason there were working disagreements. We could be disappointed if an artist had cooperated one year on an Aldeburgh project, then turned out to be unavailable the following year. Ben loathed a row, and would often go to great lengths to avoid one.'

An early working relationship was with Wystan Auden. He and Britten were both part of the GPO film unit before the war. 'I think Wystan opened up all sorts of vistas for Ben. His conversation was more stimulating than anything Ben had encountered until then. Cobwebs were blown away; he shocked Ben, and also freed him, but in the end the partnership didn't prove to be wholly successful. Wystan tended to work so far ahead of the composer when they were writing *Paul Bunyan* together that Ben found himself presented with a *fait accompli*. Their next venture was to be a Christmas oratorio. Ideas were discussed on the east coast of the United States before Ben and I left for a tour in the west. When we got back to New York, we discovered that Wystan had already completed the libretto and from Ben's point of view it was quite unsuitable for the project.

'Ben was disconsolate because he had hoped to begin writing the music. It seemed obvious that the usefulness of the partnership was at an end. From this experience, Ben learnt that in the future he must discuss every step of a work with his librettists and work in harness with them. Indeed, when it came to his next stage work, *Grimes*, almost every word was discussed with Montagu Slater, and a similar pattern was followed in collaboration with other writers.'

Britten's home life ran, in Sir Peter's words, along 'fairly sure rails'. 'Ben was no Bohemian. He adhered to a regular life, beginning with a cold bath in the morning, to whose delights he introduced me. In domestic matters he was somewhat at a loss. He could make a cup of tea, boil an egg and wash up, but not much more. If he made his bed, he usually made a mess of it. He preferred simple food to exotic. He adored the garden, but was no weeder himself. In our spare time, always too restricted, we loved to "church crawl". Ben was charmed by any new feature of architecture we discovered.

'He was religious in the general sense of acknowledging a power above greater than ourselves, but he wasn't a regular churchgoer. In his moral attitudes, he was low church, and therefore inclined to be puritanical. He had a conscience, believing in such old-fashioned virtues as honour. Strict working standards in a sense reflected strict moral ones. In short, he thought people should behave properly and not betray one another. If, to his way of thinking, they misbehaved, he did not forgive them easily. I think the key to his music lies in his moral point of view combined with his craving for lost innocence brought on by his increasing disillusionment with man.'

During his last illness, Britten was given heart by his friend's wish that he should never lose his faith in music. For a year he wrote nothing. Then, happily, he was able to resume work and produce his last few precious compositions. He had no terror of dying, no particular conviction of what might follow death. 'His greatest feeling was his sorrow at the thought of leaving me and his responsibilities. He had earlier said that he had to die first because he didn't know what he would do without me.'

So ended a devoted relationship. 'And a quite marvellous one. He made my career by all the wonderful works he wrote for me. On the other hand, he said he would not have achieved anything without me. It was established almost at once that we were very close to each other; from then on little disturbed our friendship. I like to think I returned his faith, though perhaps I could not match his wholehearted trust, faith, love.'

2
Beth Welford

Beth Welford is Britten's younger sister and always remembers her brother as being concerned for other people. Having earned a lot of money, he was determined to be generous with it. For himself, he wished for very little; indeed she thinks he could have easily lived in a hut provided he had enough to eat. Bearing in mind composers of the past who have suffered in poverty, she believes he was fortunate to have been a success while still alive, 'but he was always grateful for his good luck in that respect'.

Maybe he owed that success to his singleminded ambition, from when he was a small boy, to be a musician. Except for a passing phase when it was suggested he might be a mathematician, he had been set fair to become a musician for as long as she can remember. He was certainly brilliant at maths at his prep school, and his parents, always doubtful about his making a living at music, at least insisted that he went on at school until he was sixteen.

He started to write music before he could write words, and he never faltered from that path. He was also a born pianist. As far as his sister can remember, 'There was never any doubt that music in some form was to be Ben's future. From the age of two years he scrambled on to the piano stool, saying, "Dear pay pano," (he called himself "dear" when a child). At the age of five, before he could write words, he started to put notes of music on to paper, although of course at first they did not make any musical sense. He said later that he gave our mother these bits of paper and asked her to play them for him. Her look of horror at this request assured him that he had not as yet made real music. Not to be deterred, Ben struggled on, and before he was nine had written *real* music. Ben later arranged some of the pieces he wrote then and these became the *Simple Symphony*.

'Certainly the gods smiled on Benjamin as far as gifts were concerned. If he had not become a composer, he could equally well have been a solo pianist, a mathematician, or excelled at some sport. Alas, the one thing the gods did not give him was good health. When a small baby, he had a serious illness, and the doctors warned our parents that Benjamin would never be strong – that in fact he would probably never be able to live a normal life. In spite of this, he not only lived a normal life, he lived an abnormal one, at a tremendous pace, considering what he achieved in his sixty-three years.'

He was popular with his contemporaries and had many friends. When he was growing up, Beth was closest to him because she was nearest in age. Their sister Barbara had gone to London, brother Robert was away at school. Although Ben was the youngest in the family, she always recalls him as the wise one, teaching the others what to do, ready with good advice. He was better at tennis than Beth and tried (unsuccessfully) to teach her the violin.

Although their mother certainly spoilt her son, he was in fact 'unspoilable'. If he had been inclined that way, Beth thinks, he could have been very conceited, because he was so good at everything to which he put his mind, but he took his talents in his stride, and was always modest.

For a time, while Britten was at Gresham's School, she saw less of him but, when he went to the Royal College in London, they shared a flat in Cromwell Road. She recalls that he was frustrated by the tedium of much of his work at the college, but he stuck it out and got his LRM. There were visits to his teacher Frank Bridge, where he joined the Bridges in string quartets. During this period, he was pouring out music, writing at a tremendous pace. Then, when he went to work for the GPO film unit, Beth recalls how good the discipline was for him, as was his work at the Mercury Theatre, where he met many other young composers of the day.

When he went to America, his family were convinced that he

would remain there, and even become an American citizen. Fortunately, he thought better of it. On his return during the war, he joined Beth at the mill he owned in Snape, Suffolk, which he had asked her to live in while he was away. During his time in the US he wrote to her frequently, showing concern about his family. At first he seemed to be happy there, admiring as he did the enthusiasm of the Americans. Gradually, though, he became disenchanted both with them and with his progress there.

After about 1946 she saw less of him for a while. She had married and gone to live some twelve miles away; he was becoming well known and was in demand all over the place. At first, she thinks, he liked fame, because it marked his success, but later it became a burden to him. There are those who think he lost something by moving away from the centre of things, but Beth is not among them.

He was a strict person in the sense that he liked people to behave properly, dress conventionally, take their morals seriously. He was religious in the sense that he lived by a set of values. Their mother was active in the low church. Their father was an agnostic. On Sunday some of the family went to church with their mother, others went out in the car with the father. Their mother was musical, their father not. Britten and his mother played duets, and he accompanied her singing; she also played the viola in quartets. The children loved their mother; they looked up to their father as the disciplinarian. Britten got on well with him and shared his wry sense of humour, dedication to work and capacity for taking pains.

Britten was grateful that he had had a straightforward childhood – sleeping and eating at regular times – because it taught him to be disciplined in his work. He got up and went to bed early. He ate simply.

The upbringing was provincial, and Mrs Welford has no doubt that Wystan Auden broadened Ben's outlook. Britten's father had certainly introduced his son to literature, but Auden widened his knowledge of it enormously. For a while, Britten admired him inordinately and, even after the break, the influence remained.

Mrs Welford thinks that the impression that Ben was at odds with the world is quite mistaken. 'He was very much part of it – and wanted to take part in it.' He might be very sensitive and worry himself deeply about all the wrongs that were taking place, but he was never negative in his attitude. He worked endlessly for charity, in particular for the Save the Children Fund, for which he wrote *Children's Crusade*. He adopted children in the sense that he supported them. Professionally, he put innumerable children in touch with music. *Noyes Fludde* is dedicated to Beth's children.

In later years, she often went walking with him, and when he became ill she looked after him until he had a nurse. While it was sad to see him so incapacitated, it was marvellous to be with him. He showed amazing courage, and could still laugh and joke. He was determined to cheer up any other person who was with him.

'To me, Ben was a very loving brother; to my children, a dear kind uncle – they were so fond of him. In spite of pressure of work, Ben always had time to stop and listen to any problem we might have and help if he could in some way or other. He had so much compassion for everyone, also humour and a great deal of fun.'

3
John and Myfanwy Piper

Joan Piper's friendship with Benjamin Britten began, developed and strengthened through their working together. They worked together because they both had a passion for a unity of the arts in the theatre. What sounded good must look good; what made musical sense must make visual and poetic sense as well. It was an ideal that was inspired, for those born before the First World War, by the Diaghilev Ballet – either directly, or through other creative artists under its influence. Rupert Doone was one of those. He had been a friend of Diaghilev and a dancer in his ballet; when he had to stop dancing through illness, he turned his attention to production. In order to do what he wanted in the theatre, he had to gather together his own group of artists and run his own show. This was the Group Theatre, started in the early thirties. Wystan Auden, Louis MacNeice, Stephen Spender, Robert Medley, Christopher Isherwood, Benjamin Britten and Hedli Anderson, amongst other singers and actors, were founder members. John Piper joined in 1935, and in 1936, when the Group was suffering some internal squabbles and severe financial anxiety there was a weekend conference (ending in a large party) at Fawley Bottom, the Piper's house near Henley. It was not an easy occasion; a lot of emotion, a lot of intellectual bullying and consultations in separate rooms. But a lot of enjoyment too. Britten and Auden played 'Night and Day' four-handed on the piano; Piper and Britten discussed music and musicians – particularly Poulenc, an enthusiasm they shared; Britten smoked his first and (and only?) cigarette in the garden – not so enjoyable.

Of the personalities at that gathering, Auden was clearly the most accomplished in getting his own way. He dominated and expected to, but because he was also already acknowledged as a very good poet, his influence was serious and far-reaching.

Britten's understanding of the power and the magic of words and his excitement is selling them had already been very much stimulated by Auden. Their work together was demanding, absorbing and useful to them both. When Auden went with Isherwood to America in 1939 Britten was pesuaded to follow them. Piper thinks that Auden's influence was so strong that it was almost impossible to resist. William Coldstream received the same command. But both Britten and Coldstream came back.

Although they corresponded during the war, Britten and Piper did not collaborate until, after the production of *Peter Grimes* at Sadler's Wells in 1946, the composer began work on *The Rape of Lucretia* and asked Piper to design it. He had, meanwhile, designed *The Quest*, a ballet with music by William Walton and choreography by Frederick Ashton, and *Oedipus Rex*, with Laurence Olivier and the Old Vic Company, then playing, like the Sadler's Wells Ballet, at the New Theatre.

The Rape of Lucretia was produced at Glyndebourne in the summer of 1947. The working relationship between composer and painter set the pattern for all future collaborations and for their friendship: a mutual trust and respect, an ability to learn from each other and to accommodate the demands of their respective trades. John, with his passion fot the ballet, was inclined to think of design in terms of the great and splendid Diaghilev backcloths. But for opera the stage must be furnished. Britten was very practical: 'What is going to happen here, in the first act, when this character has to move [or sit, or exit]? I can't write the music until I can visualize the action!' Although he had a proper dislike of realism and the box set, this need to be specific did lead to prolonged discussion. For example, in *The Turn of the Screw* the governess arrives by coach, and Ben wanted the coach to be seen – not from a desire for inappropriate realism, but because he was afraid that the music alone would not get it across to an audience unfamiliar with the musical idiom and with the understated abstraction of the stage picture. But it was precisely this last quality that would not absorb a coach. So there had to be persuasion and adjustment. The producer, Basil Coleman, had the brilliant idea of using the motions of someone sitting in a coach, and the merest whisper of a wheel and a door panel in the painted gauze settled the issue to everyone's satisfaction.

It was the rule at Glyndebourne that productions were made there, with everyone living in the house or in the neighbourhood for several weeks before the opening night. This is an ideal way to produce a properly rehearsed whole – with no waiting about because someone has gone to Manchester or Berlin. In spite of the inevitable contretemps when so many strong personalities are gathered together for so long, rehearsing for *The Rape of Lucretia* was a happy time. The happiness was shattered when, after the dress rehearsal, John Christie called a meeting of producer (Eric Crozier), librettist (Ronald Duncan), designer, cast and composer and told them that the whole work was absurd and inadequate, and the music incomprehensible; he pointed out that the arches in the set hadn't even got reveals. It was this insensitive treatment, coming together with the obvious advantages of the working conditions, that determined Britten, Peter Pears and Eric Crozier to found an opera group that would be responsible for its own productions; it would be based at Aldeburgh, where productions would be made, rehearsed and when possible performed, independently of other organizations. So the English Opera Group came into being. John was asked to be the artistic adviser.

The Rape of Lucretia was the beginning of a life-long involvement and friendship for both families. It was at Glyndebourne that John's wife Myfanwy first learnt to listen to Ben's music, to notice what happened to words that are sung, and to understand, through many talks with him, the difficulties that beset composers and writers when their work comes together – she did not realize that this experience would come in useful later. After *Lucretia*, John designed all Ben's operas (for their first production) except the three Church Parables. Of them all perhaps he enjoyed most *The Turn of the Screw*, *A Midsummer*

Night's Dream and *Death in Venice*. This work meant many visits to Aldeburgh, sometimes very short, when the Pipers stayed with Ben and Peter, and sometimes, when a production was in progress, for much longer, when they took a house. John became devoted to Ben and learnt an enormous amount from him – not only about music, but about life, about being an artist, about integrity, about tolerance and intolerance too. They were both humble before other peoples skills, and both took enormous trouble when anyone wanted help with his own work. They respected each other's habits, which were very different. Because he was so vulnerable, Britten built up a close circle of associates as protection against the world and for his privacy. Wounds inflicted did not easily heal. It was easy to offend him and people who broke his own code of behaviour were not easily forgiven. He was a little formal in his way of living, courteous in an old-fashioned way, almost over-polite. He found it difficult to relax, except when he played games for exercise – a thing that John never did (except table tennis) – or went for long walks along the marshes, or drove through the Suffolk lanes looking at old churches, which he loved. This common passion with John was an endless source of pleasure. Between bouts of hard work, difficult negotiations or serious personal problems, Britten would talk, on these church-crawling expeditions, about the difficulties and complexities of his life and receive sympathetic and impartial advice; at the same time, he would come to appreciate some church or place that he had seen before but with different eyes, or they would both enjoy the excitement of seeing somewhere completely new to them. There was never any rift, or even coolness, between them.

The need for support was certainly very real. It was remarkable how beastly people could be: about his way of life, about his having been a conscientious objector (let alone going to the States for two years) and about his work. The commissioning of *Gloriana* by Covent Garden for performance during the Coronation celebrations caused a lot of backstairs gossip, extremely painful to the composer and nearly disastrous for the general administrator.

John enjoyed and admired *Gloriana* and thinks that it is a much underrated work. But it was by far the most time-consuming of any work for the stage that he had done. Work on the costumes alone took months. In fact, it was the last time that he undertook to design costumes as well as sets, except for in *The Turn of the Screw*.

The Turn of the Screw was the first opera in which both John and Myfanwy were involved. When Ben began to think of it as a subject, he remembered that Myfanwy had suggested it as a possible film (when Ben was being pressed unsuccessfully to do one), so he asked if she would think about how it might he treated, with the idea that someone more professional, like William Plomer, might be called in to write the script. But ideas flowed and they decided to do without anyone else. She had some misgivings because of her lack of musical knowledge, but what she had learnt from listening to so many rehearsals of so many works helped to give her confidence. Words mattered, and Ben set them as if they mattered and were meant to be heard. As she wrote in *The Operas of Benjamin Britten*[1] she knew that 'nothing can be slurred over in a fine flourish of sound, nothing shrugged off as operatic licence'. She had developed an instinctive feeling for what words might sound like when he set them. It was the experience of his music as much as her own sensitivity that made it possible for her to have a rapport with his work. It was typical of him that, once he had decided to ask her to do the whole work, he accepted her as a professional. His own theatrical experience and expertise were there to help and to enrich, not to correct or lay down the law. Much of their discussion was done by letter or immensely long telephone conversations, but sometimes she would go briefly to Aldeburgh. These visits would have been more frequent had she not been needed at home with her children. It was not until much later that she realized how frustrating her lack of immediate availability had been and with what ungrumbling patience (to her at least) Ben had put up with it.

In 1953 there were fewer very young singers (especially girls)

[1] Hamish Hamilton, 1979.

than today, and they were far less sophisticated musically. Ben thought that whichever boy sang the part of Miles would need a great deal of musical support from Flora and that therefore Flora would have to be sung by an experienced soprano – they would just have to find one small enough not to look absurd. In the end the part was written for Olive Dyer, well known as a singer of child parts. She was tiny, and though not young carried it off with immense verve. It was in fact sung with great success by a teenage girl in the Kent Opera's 1980 production – almost inconceivable twenty-five years ago. Myfanwy has wondered if, had Ben been writing today he would have written Flora's part to be sung by another boy. They did discuss the possibility at the time but rejected it. It was a tempting idea, but it is doubtful if it could have worked with only six singers in all.

Towards the end of the rehearsal period, Ben would play the completed piano score, or part of it, to those involved, somehow managing to convey a complete orchestra with his hands and all the voices in his rather strange low voice. Those who were used to it got to know what the finished work would sound like. There were wonderfully funny moments: a rendering of the Lion's part from *A Midsummer Night's Dream* remains indelibly in the mind. One could never have enough of these marvellously explanatory performances. *The Turn of the Screw* was given one hot June evening at Fawley Bottom. At the climax of Act 1 the piano was suddenly joined by violent and unexpected thunderclaps.

The Turn of the Screw had been commissioned by the Fenice Theatre in Venice and was first performed in an Italian translation. Everyone concerned worked there for two or three weeks. Those long hot September days, full of nervous anticipation, relieved by an occasional swim in the Lido, provided an insight into the moods and secrets and oppressions of the city that were to be reinforced by further visits and used to the full in the writing and designing of *Death in Venice*.

It was fifteen years before Myfanwy worked again with Ben, although they had discussed ideas for a short opera for New York television which came to nothing. One of the stories discussed was Henry James's *Owen Wingrave* and Britten returned to that when asked for a work for BBC Television. By this time, Myfanwy felt that her friendship with him was secure on a personal, as well as a professional, level. It made differences of opinion easier – though they were usually in agreement. She felt able almost to bully him about his dislike of Kate and to persuade him to see that she was just as much a victim of upbringing as Owen, though not so capable of rebellion.

Writing *Owen Wingrave* was an immense pleasure. Myfanwy was free of her family and so more easily available; she had strong feelings about her work, but she never felt it more important than the use to which it was being put, since she was not a poet or writer in her own right. Adaptations or changes were a natural part of the job. During the writing of *Owen Wingrave*, and later *Death in Venice*, she was constantly amazed by the sureness of Ben's theatrical inventiveness. For instance, the scene at the end of *Death in Venice* where the manager and porter exchange sharp words, and the manager shows himself as the manipulator of the denouement, was written entirely at his instigation – and, as always, he was right.

While *Owen Wingrave* was still being telerecorded at Snape, Ben asked her if she would think about writing *Death in Venice*. About six weeks after that, in January 1970, the Pipers set off for a working holiday in France with Ben and Peter. It was the culmination of all the years they had known each other, and of their working together. John drove, Peter map-read and the other two analysed Thomas Mann's story and put it into a possible operatic shape. There were visits to Romanesque churches – old favourites and unknown ones too – and a series of prolonged and splendid meals. There was a lot of talk. Ben never slept very long at night and he said that among the books by his bed he always had a volume of Haydn quartets: 'For someone who reads music easily it is a complete autobiography, a complete revelation of the man.'

The following October there was another journey, this time to Venice. They had all been several times since *The Turn of the Screw*, but never together. They walked about the streets and squares, listened to the gondoliers' cries – to hear authentic ones they had to search out one of the few remaining families who still knew, but did not habitually use, the old terms – and

John made many drawings.

It was on those journeys, and during the many visits to Aldeburgh in the last years of Britten's life, that the Pipers came to understand the inevitability of their association. Their friendship had been long and rewarding; it was tragic that, at the moment of greatest fruition, it had to end.

4

Marion Thorpe

Marion Thorpe, or Marion Stein as she then was, believes that she first met Britten in Vienna during the 1930s when the youthful composer went there to meet Alban Berg. She was herself then too young to remember the occasion, but her father, the distinguished musicologist Erwin Stein (also a close friend of Britten), often talked about it to her. Her own first recollection of encountering him was in 1938, at the first performance of *A Ballad of Heroes* at the Queen's Hall. Britten swore that Marion curtseyed to him in the Green Room after the concert – in the best central European tradition.

After Britten returned from the United States in 1942, he was greatly encouraged by Stein, the music editor of the composer's current publisher, Boosey and Hawkes. Their musical association was based on similar tastes, both being admirers of Mahler and Berg (*Wozzeck* being in some ways a model for Britten), among others. Naturally Marion was present at all of those historic premieres of Britten's works during the Second World War and those just after it, such as the *Michelangelo Sonnets* and the *Serenade*, which offered balm in those bleak years.

There were visits for holidays to Snape, where Britten lived at the time. Works were played through by the composer and Stein, and Britten's creative force produced a tremendous frisson of excitement. Mrs Thorpe feels that she was able to get to know the pieces from the inside even before the first performances. As a teenager, she found Britten an exciting personality, not only as a composer but also as a pianist. As a player herself, she often joined him in duets, particularly after Britten and Pears came to share a home with her family in

London. That came about through a fire, unconnected with the war, at the Steins' flat. At the time, incidentally, the autograph score of *Peter Grimes* had been in the flat, and she believes that it still bears watermarks from the aftermath of that fire. It was the first thing to be saved.

The Steins had nowhere to sleep on the night after the fire, so they rang Britten, who suggested they should come to the flat in St John's Wood High Street where Pears and Britten then had their London home. It was above the Home and Colonial Stores (long since departed), and being on three floors was capacious enough to house the Steins as well. (Marion recalls in passing that Tippett was another visitor at the time.) The arrangement took on some permanency for a good reason: Britten was dissatisfied with his housekeeper and Mrs Stein agreed to take on her duties – a satisfactory arrangement for all concerned. For Marion, who was just at the end of her school career, it was a happy time, though when Britten was at home working she would be required to go elsewhere to practise – often to Basil Douglas's home at Primrose Hill. Apart from anything else, she would have been tense and unable to play if she knew Britten had been listening to her.

The great event of this time, of course, was the preparation of *Peter Grimes*. There was a feeling of expectancy and an anticipation of an auspicious premiere at the rehearsals Marion attended, in spite of the tensions, described vividly by Joan Cross (q.v.), which were caused by the ructions in the Sadler's Wells Company. The war was coming to an end; and *Peter Grimes* was to an extent indicative of the lifting clouds. Suddenly there seemed to be a fully fledged British opera composer. Ralph Hawkes deserves much credit for furthering Britten's works; he was the driving force in the firm of Boosey and Hawkes at the time, and he saw to it that the work came to fruition. This and his courage helped not only the dissemination of Britten's work but also that of Stravinsky and Bartók. Marion still recalls the party thrown by Hawkes at the Savoy after the first night, which was attended by all musical London; she wore her first long dress at it, which had been given to her by her former headmistress!

After the party an amusing incident occurred. It was very late, and outside the back of the Home and Colonial some stray cats were scrounging and caterwauling. Marion had determined to throw something on the wretched creatures from her room on the first floor. As she did so, a pail of water descended from above, from Britten's room, drenching her! 'Complete hysterics ensued; nobody could sleep. Many, many years later, at a performance of *Grimes* at Covent Garden after Britten's operation, he rather touchingly reminded me of the episode of the cats. It was indicative of his great sense of humour.'

During these formative years of her life, Marion remembers vividly the demands for high standards made by Britten on her and others. He expected and got the best out of people but, on the other hand, if people demanded too much of him musically or personally he did not like it. He had fewer skins than most people, and one had to be careful of what one said or did not say to him. Her friendship with him was not stilted, but she realized its limits.

She was very much concerned in the years following *Grimes* with the formation of the Aldeburgh Festival and the English Opera Group. Discussions about their inception took place first at St John's Wood, then at a larger home, in Oxford Square, where the Steins, Britten and Pears again shared quarters, the ménage working successfully once more. Eric Crozier, Joan Cross, John Piper and Ronald Duncan were frequent visitors to the house. As is well known, Britten was concerned to break away from the limitation of larger, institutional opera companies, partly because he was very practical and wanted to tailor his material to particular forces. A small company would be more mobile and rehearsals simpler, and the results would be under his direct control. Then the strains of the Glyndebourne seasons, described elsewhere, decided him and Pears to create their own festival. There was enough local support to make the idea of music at home, as it were, feasible. There was freedom from the harassment of the big world, a freedom for them to do their own thing.

Britten and Pears made one further move with the Stein family – to Melbury Road in Kensington (in the meantime

Marion had married), before moving, in 1951, to Chester Square, their own home. After Marion married George Harewood, her friendship with Britten and Pears remained just as close. They stayed at Harewood House, and there were holidays together, to France, Switzerland and Ireland. It was during some of these holidays that Britten was thinking about another large-scale opera. He had in mind a work with a national feeling to it, his *Bartered Bride* as it were. With the Coronation in the offing, he had the idea of a celebration of the first Elizabeth, and so *Gloriana* was created; it was performed the following year.

With hindsight, Mrs Thorpe can see that the Coronation was the wrong occasion for that particular work, though it did not seem so at the time. She recalls that there seemed hardly a musical person in sight at the premiere, apart from the composer's friends – and critics, who were anything but sympathetic at that time to the piece. Britten, as ever sensitive to criticism, was deeply hurt by the reactions of public and press. He himself always knew where the faults were in his works and where he had failed to solve a technical problem, but those were never the ones alighted on by his critics.

Marion attended the rehearsals for *The Turn of the Screw* in Venice in 1954, a work that she found difficult at first. Come the first night, she found it utterly convincing.

At recitals, she used to turn pages for Britten in his role as executant, a nerve-racking experience, not because he was fussy about how one did it, like some pianists, but because he was so nervous himself before a concert, and his tensions were often communicated to others – it was almost as if one was about to play oneself on the platform. Such near proximity to him on the platform, in addition to the fact that she is a pianist herself, makes Marion Thorpe an ideal person to judge his merits as a player. The unique kind of sound he made amazed her, and his sonority has almost become a criterion by which she judges others. In spite of the fact that he hardly ever practised, everything seemed to come to Britten quite naturally. In duos with Clifford Curzon, it was Curzon who worked out his fingering to the last degree. This worried Britten because, if he was urged to think about such technical problems, if he had to work out fingering, he simply would not be able to play at all; he was primarily an instinctive pianist. His playing went straight from his musical brain to his fingers without hindrance.

As a personal friend to Mrs Thorpe, he could not have been more considerate. Whenever she had any troubles, she could turn to him. She recalls on one occasion speaking to him on the phone; a few moments after she had put it down, he rang back to ask if she was all right because he felt instinctively that something was wrong. If she had some good news to tell him, he guessed what it would be before words were spoken. This was indicative of his general concern about other people – whether they were close friends, young musicians, or anyone else. He was generous in that respect not only with his time but also with financial help.

Yet the paradox is that he was a very private person who liked to be by himself or in his small circle of friends. That, she considers, may have been because of the tenseness in his make-up which in turn often made him ill. The tenseness was the product of the extraordinarily busy life he led, touring to give recitals with Pears when he was not composing. He felt, though, that he must perform as well as write because it would keep him in contact with musical life. Therefore, he was at times over-stretching himself. He was genuinely very ill on several occasions, including once before the *Spring Symphony* and then later when he had a major operation for diverticulitis; these were both well before his heart ailment. Perhaps his body was not able to cope with the tremendous amount of creative activity that he was involved in, not to mention the minute organization of the festival. There, incidentally, he would take a close interest in every detail, always remaining very conscious of practicalities.

This sense of what was possible was carried over into his writing for a singer or an instrumentalist. He knew, often better that the artist concerned, what could be achieved. He hated the romantic idea of the composer who sits there waiting for inspiration. For him, writing was a hard, down-to-earth matter, and he disciplined himself to a strict régime. He would work right through the morning, then walk until tea, then between tea and dinner he would tend to spend his time on orchestration, or some compositional matter that was more mundane than actually creating. He never waited for inspiration. If there was a difficulty he would pace about trying to overcome it. He would then almost regret that he did not smoke (although he hated smokers), because he thought that might help when the creative process was proving recalcitrant.

Special pieces were written for Marion and her family – a wedding anthem for her marriage to Lord Harewood, *The Rape of Lucretia* for her father. *Billy Budd* is dedicated to her and Lord Harewood, as is *Night Piece*, one of the few of his works for piano alone, which was written for the first Leeds Competition.

Marion went with Britten to Russia for the premieres of the *Cello Symphony* in Moscow and Leningrad. Mrs Thorpe remembers him trying to learn at least 'one, two, three, four' in Russian so that he could direct the Russian orchestra. That was a time of great happiness, because Britten established a close rapport with Rostropovich and his wife, Galina Vishnevskaya, and cemented his friendship with Shostakovich, who later dedicated his fourteenth symphony to Britten. On one occasion in the early seventies Shostakovich, on a visit to this country, made a special detour with his wife to come to Aldeburgh. He stayed at the Uplands hotel, and Mrs Thorpe gave a small dinner party for them. She also remembers visiting his flat with Britten in Moscow and discussions about their latest pieces. Britten admired something Shostakovich played on the piano at which Shostakovich, who had learnt a little English for the occasion, said, 'No, no; you great composer, I little composer.' Mrs Thorpe thinks there was deep understanding between the two composers. The relationship between Rostropovich and Britten was one of affectionate friendship and mutual admiration. Britten also admired Vishnevsakaya's voice and, besides *The Poet's Echo*, would have liked to bring to fruition the idea of writing *Anna Karenina* for her. Captivated by her personality, he could vividly see her in that role.

Apropos the music itself, Marion Thorpe perhaps appreciates

more than anything its structure. Britten knew how to build a piece and where to place the climaxes, and in general he had an innate feeling for pace. 'When you know the works well, you know which moments will affect you deeply – and they do not fail to do so at each hearing.

'The clarity of texture, the skilful and often original use of instruments or voices makes all his music immediately recognizable – as one would with Mahler or Schubert, one knows at once "this is Britten", Yet, given the technical mastery, it is the humanity of his music that is so profoundly moving. The depth of his insight into human emotion, the understanding and compassion expressed through the music – these are the lasting qualities. He often said, "I want to be useful"; he wanted his music used to communicate – and that he certainly achieved.'

5

Sir Lennox Berkeley

Sir Lennox Berkeley, who knew Britten particularly well during the early part of his life as a composer, first met him at a festival of contemporary music at Barcelona in 1937. Berkeley and Britten were the only British composers who were represented in the programmes. They immediately became good friends. Berkeley had not encountered Britten until then as he had been living with his mother in the South of France, and was out of contact with events in England. Back in his own country Berkeley shared living quarters with Britten in part of the old mill at Snape. Though mainly based in London, Berkeley managed to spend weekends at Snape, where he soon got to know Britten very well. They discussed music at length and had a good deal in common, while by no means always finding themselves in agreement. Both were also busy writing music, particularly scores for radio programmes.

Berkeley found Britten charming, simple, straightforward – and extremely talented. He also realized that his younger colleague's musical ability went far beyond his own, and found that this was to his advantage because he was able to learn from Britten, although there is no doubt that Britten also picked up some ideas from him. Britten was very open to the influence of the French composers with whom Berkeley had worked and studied – that is obvious in *Les Illuminations*, which was being composed at that time. Also being written during the period of their closest collaboration was the piano concerto, which is dedicated to Berkeley, who felt that Britten played the piano so well that he ought to write a work for the instrument. Although Berkeley does not consider it one of Britten's best works, the concerto made a considerable impression at its first performance – at the Proms – partly because here was a young composer actually playing his own new work. The end of this association came when Britten left for the United States just before the Second World War.

Berkeley met Britten again soon after his return when he received a call from the composer, who said he had a piece he wanted to show him. Berkeley went up to the flat in St John's Wood, and Britten played through the whole of the first act of *Peter Grimes*. Berkeley had surmised it was something important but was not quite prepared for this, although he believed, even before the war, that Britten was capable of something as large-scale as that he heard. Britten covered the orchestral part thoroughly on the piano while also singing many of the vocal parts as he went along. The impact on Berkeley of the first performance, when it came, was enormous.

After that, Britten's concentration on composing and the many demands on his time meant that he saw less of Berkeley, although they were frequently in contact, exchanging views. Berkeley often attended the Aldeburgh Festival where many of his works were heard. His operas *A Dinner Engagement, Ruth* and *Castaway* were given premieres by the English Opera Group.

Berkeley thinks that, as the years went by, Britten became more set in his ways, and as a composer he was difficult to argue with once he had his ideas on paper. He believed he had it right by the time he had got that far – and was usually proved correct. That was what made him so sensitive to criticism: he hated people not to appreciate what he had achieved or indeed to fail to understand it. As a fellow creative artist, Berkeley understands that attitude – a very natural one. In later years he heard that Britten could be stubborn, even opinionated, although he himself never experienced anything but agreeable charm.

With regard to the works, Berkeley considers *The Turn of the Screw* Britten's masterpiece; he thinks it is an almost perfect composition, which indicates a full flowering of Britten's gifts, and that it was the apex of the whole central period, the richest in its rewards. *A Midsummer Night's Dream* and the *War Requiem* also belong to that period and, in Berkeley's opinion, are of comparable standard. Together they demonstrate the breadth and variety of Britten's genius. If these works were the most generous in their accomplishments, some of the late ones, such as *Death in Venice* and the third quartet, show an advance into what looked as if it might be a new refinement of Britten's idiom. Although on the whole, he needed a text to stimulate his inspirations, his last string quartet may well become accepted as the masterpiece of his later manner.

Yet, at the time before the war when Berkeley knew him best, it was by no means certain Britten would become an opera composer. He had certainly determined to write one work in that field, but he might as easily have concentrated on instrumental music. It was the success of *Grimes* that stimulated him to write more opera.

Britten wrote easily in those early years, but he later told Berkeley that he was composing much more slowly because he had become more self-critical. Berkeley thinks that it would have been easy for Britten always to continue to write in the successful style he had worked out for himself, but that at each stage of his creative life he sought something new, and tried to fashion his style afresh. He felt that he must probe ever deeper into his creative springs, but, as he did so, composing became harder for him.

Britten was not influenced so much by his contemporaries as by composers of the past, particularly Mahler and Berg. Berkeley thinks that all composers are to some extent indebted to the great that have gone before. Many share, though, a special affection for Mozart. Although renowned for his dislike of Brahms (which Berkeley did not share), Britten admitted to Berkeley that he had much admired that composer when at school. Even in the early days he was drawn to Schumann and Tchaikovsky, with a particular love of the latter's *Romeo and Juliet* and *Francesca da Rimini*. In general, he was very well acquainted with a great deal of music and could discuss the scores in detail. He could also retain a large amount of music in his head, his own included.

He composed away from the piano, but would always try out

what he had written as soon as he could, going over it meticulously, note by note, because he did not always trust what he had thought out in his mind. Indeed when he tried pieces at the piano, he would often make substantial corrections. Even so, he was more adept than most composers at getting things right the first time.

Britten conducted the first London performance of Sir Lennox's *Stabat Mater* with the English Opera Group. Booked to give a concert at Zurich, the EOG, or rather Britten, wanted a new work for the occasion. The *Stabat Mater* was the result, using the EOG solo singers and players. This appears to be the only time he conducted any of Berkeley's music.

6

Peter Schidlof

After Peter Schidlof came to Britain with his family in 1938, he was billeted at Southwold, Suffolk, where he met the music staff of a girls' school there. One of the staff introduced him to the cellist Michel Cherniavsky, who had had a famous trio. Cherniavsky was then living at Saxmundham, and knew Britten, who was at the mill at Snape, and he often played with the composer. Schidlof accompanied Cherniavsky on a visit. Immediately Schidlof felt that he was in the presence of someone special, even though he then knew very little about him, and hardly spoke any English.

Schidlof next came into contact with Britten at Morley College, when Pears sang *Les Illuminations*. Soon after that he found himself the viola player in the chamber orchestra assembled for the first performances of *The Rape of Lucretia* at Glyndebourne. While Ansermet was the conductor, Schidlof recalls Britten giving very precise instructions about how he wanted his score played. At once it was evident to him just how fine was Britten's ear. When the production was taken to Holland, Britten took over as conductor, and the work, in Schidlof's opinion, went much more easily.

Soon after this, the Amadeus Quartet was formed, and its members invited to the newborn Aldeburgh Festival. Quite often Britten joined them as pianist. In the pieces which they played together, Britten's influence on their interpretation was paramount. Sometimes, indeed, the young Amadeus were attempting them for the first time with his encouragement. He would also offer his opinion on the string works: Schidlof recalls good advice about Schubert's *Death and the Maiden*. His understanding of everything was from a composer's point of view, and so was both refreshing and instructive for the Amadeus. He would dare things that no one else would dare. In the works with piano, he came in having practised very little and played them in a revelatory manner. Britten and Schidlof cooperated not only at the festival but in London and abroad. One of the places they visited was Schloss Elmau near Garmisch-Partenkirchen in Bavaria where every winter there used to be an English-German week. There Britten was much more accessible than at Aldeburgh and proved pleasant company.

In the repertory of the Amadeus at that time was Britten's own second quartet. He was helpful about interpretation: the Chaconne was being taken too fast, the semiquavers there should be shorter, for example. At the end of Britten's life came the third quartet, which is dedicated to the Amadeus. It had been long promised, as had a concerto for quartet and orchestra that remained, alas, uncomposed. As far as the quartet itself is concerned, Britten said a few years before he wrote it that he had it all in his head, but simply had not found the time to write it down. Then suddenly, without any advance warning, Peter Pears told the Amadeus that it had been written; they could hardly believe the good news.

The Amadeus went to the Red House to study the quartet with Britten. As he was already weak, it was possible only to work for twenty minutes or so at a session, but his ear was as keen as ever, his spirit quite unbroken. He listened to their playing with all the old intensity and it was impossible for them to get away with anything. Again his instructions were very precise about where to make a slight rubato, when to move forward just a little bit more quickly. Yet he always told them that he had complete faith and trust in their ability to carry out his demands. The occasions were all the more moving because somehow Britten had a premonition that he would not be present to hear the first performance. Schidlof feels that the work is a true epilogue to Britten's career.

Schidlof is appreciative of the law and order of Britten's music in today's lawless musical world. Every bar 'sound' has a musical purpose and projection. There are no unwanted noises. Everything harmonizes.

Besides his quartet work with Britten, Schidlof recalls a performance together with Norbert Brainin of Mozart's *Sinfonia Concertante*. To play that music with him was sheer delight. A little while later, at Christmas, Schidlof received a Christmas card on which Britten had written, 'What Mozart!'. Hearing him conduct was also an amazing experience for it imparted a freshness to scores that made them sound like new. It was as if they were being played for the first time, whether they were the works of Bach, Mozart or Tchaikovsky. However, Britten could be very despondent if something had not worked as he wished, although he was very forgiving if someone made a mistake. On one occasion in the scherzo of Britten's second quartet, which the Amadeus played very fast, Schidlof remember getting out of time – he was shattered; but Britten laughed off the incident.

Britten was, of course, very sympathetic to Schidlof as a fellow viola player. On one occasion the Amadeus learnt the Smetana quartet specially for the festival at Britten's request, and Schidlof can recall him saying that he should play his part as loud as possible. One unforgettable experience was playing Britten's own *Lachrymae* with the composer at the piano. 'Nobody can play the tremolos at the beginning as he played them, to get the texture right, and he achieved this with virtually no difficulty or practice.'

On another occasion, Britten asked the Amadeus to learn Shostakovich's thirteenth quartet for the festival, as the composer was coming. In the event he did not arrive, but the quartet went ahead. Britten was concerned for Schidlof as he knew the viola part went very high, but Schidlof said it would present no problem for him. After listening intently, Britten said that he was amazed that in fact the relevant passages came off. Schidlof said, 'I told you so.'

Schidlof is certain that Britten was the greatest man the members of the quartet have encountered in their long career, the most profound musician, and the kindest person.

7
Sir Clifford Curzon

Curzon met Benjamin Britten and Peter Pears on their return from the United States in 1942; it was pacifism which drew them together, their supranational feeling and conviction leading all three to be prepared for the hardships of the period while being unwilling to kill people. Curzon was able to introduce them to the Peace Pledge Union, the movement started by the noted pacifist, the Rev. Dick Sheppard.

On first meeting Britten, Curzon was struck by his refinement, and by his quietly civilized attitude to everything. His manner, and particularly his very distinctive speaking voice, revealed much about him. A two-piano partnership quickly grew out of their friendship, and they achieved an immediate rapport of hands and minds, which, from Curzon's home, moved out on to the concert platform. At that time Boosey and Hawkes were running an annual series of concerts, and it seemed quite natural for Curzon and Britten to take part, particularly as Britten's *Scottish Ballad* for two pianos and orchestra was awaiting its first London performance at the Proms.

Sir Clifford recalls how he and his wife (harpsichordist Lucille Wallace) introduced Benjamin Britten to the paintings of Matthew Smith, the famous artist – paintings which might be considered in a sense 'un-Ben-like', being strongly coloured and voluptuous while he tended to be spare and fine. Only a day or so later Britten was able to describe something as being very much in the style of this artist. Such quickness of adjustment and perception is an example of his eclecticism in regard to unfamiliar things. And he could be equally prompt in his reactions to people – to the point where he could show surprisingly different characteristics when a third person appeared.

His piano playing too contained surprises: Sir Clifford remembers that the great B flat minor Scherzo of Chopin, which takes an extraordinary pianist to play at all, figured in his early days as his solo warhorse in programmes with other artists. It is a measure of Britten's skill, and of his affinity with Chopin, that he chose to play this demanding work. He was inclined to fuss unduly over what he felt to be his technical shortcomings, but piano virtuosity in others fascinated him. He was always asking Curzon to play Liszt's *Mephisto Waltz* to him; and he continually took Sir Clifford to task for not including more Chopin in his programmes. Daring to send Ben first editions of Liszt's transcriptions of some Schubert songs for his fiftieth birthday present, Sir Clifford was delighted (and relieved) to know from his enthusiastic acknowledgement that they were 'something from which we all can learn'.

Britten was indeed always ready for new musical experiences and influences. Curzon remembers when he and his wife introduced him more closely to the delights of the harpsichord, and in particular to the art of one of their great teachers, Wanda Landowska. There was a time, indeed, when Britten appeared to be quite obsessed by Landowska's magisterial recording of Bach's *Chromatic Fantasia and Fugue*, and that alone commended him to the Curzons in those early days. When Lucille Wallace was asked by Sir Henry Wood to play Haydn's D major concerto at a Prom, Britten supplied cadenzas for the occasion, and this appears to have been the earliest instance of his writing for the harpsichord. Britten took infinite pains to make sure that he understood the possibilities of Lucille Wallace's Pleyel harpsichord. Curzon has given these manuscripts to the Britten–Pears library at Aldeburgh.

As a player himself, Britten was undoubtedly marked by his being a great composer. As a very conscious musician, he was bound to realize, better than a player who is just a pianist, the structural underpinnings of a piece of music. And he would worry as much about the shaping of a phrase of a fellow composer's music as he would about one of his own. Indeed, his sense of form was always exceptional, and it contributed greatly to the astonishing clarity of his playing.

Even where he was not in complete sympathy with a composer, as with Brahms, he could still show generous admiration. For instance, one year at Aldeburgh Curzon partnered Pears in part of a Brahms recital before playing the piano sonata (Op. 5) himself. Afterwards, Britten congratulated Curzon on making clear the relationship of the themes in the last movement – a relationship which Ben said he had never understood, and had even considered impossible to bring off in performance. Similarly, he confessed that he had never been able to unravel the arithmetic of the frequent changes in time signatures and the subdivisions of note values in the second movement of Beethoven's sonata (Op. 111). All this was part of his patent honesty where anything to do with music was concerned; and it was always an open secret that he was unable to be a true friend of anyone whose work he could not respect. Britten's admissions to Curzon are indications of his directness and simplicity; and they were of course delivered with that immense charm with which he was able to voice strong opinions. And so there were many occasions on which revealing views were exchanged. But Britten could never be persuaded to give unconsidered ones, especially about music. When asked after a rehearsal for the first performance of Alan Rawsthorne's second piano concerto for his views of the work, he said, honestly and sensibly, that he was unable to comment on it, 'because as yet I do not know my way about it'. But, once he had made up his mind, he was very firm in his judgements.

His exceptional abilities at the piano make it all the more conjectural why he himself was not inspired to write very much for the instrument other than accompaniments to his songs. Perhaps, Curzon suggests, the stimulus of a book or poem set off his creative processes most easily, and that onomatopoeia played an important part. Nevertheless, there is some ravishing music for solo piano; for example, 'Sailing' (which Curzon persuaded Ben to re-title from the somehow slightly pompous original, 'Yachting'); and 'Night', both from the *Holiday Diary*; as well as the much later *Nocturne*, written as a compulsory study for the entrants to the first Leeds Piano Competition. In these, as in the splendid two-piano pieces, he created as distinctive an atmosphere as he did in his other music; but for the most part his writing for solo piano is not his most idiomatic.

Later, when they no longer played together regularly, Curzon and Britten met less often; but, whenever Curzon appeared at the Aldeburgh Festival, the friendship was easily renewed; an artist would be greeted by Britten on arrival at his hotel, and a meal at the Red House was customary. Britten was the lodestar for everyone's guidance, and his presence was always felt. His motto seemed similar to the one Leschetizky taught to his pupils: '*Keine Kunst ohne Leben, kein Leben ohne Kunst*' (No art without life, no life without art). It is surely incorrect to say that Britten wanted to withdraw from the world, and to spend all his time composing. 'Without sacrificing any of the necessary dedication to composing, Ben enjoyed wordly pursuits: he was eager for exchanges with literary people and other friends in the arts – the stimulus of related talents. His own particular art could not be divorced from that world in which he was ever anxious to be of service.'

8
Imogen Holst [1]

When the editor of the *Musical Times* asked me to set down some of my 'impressions and memories' of Benjamin Britten, I decided that the most practical contribution I could make would be to mention a few of the things I learnt while working for him.

It is difficult to describe his energy, which always left the rest of us far behind. He could go straight from a rehearsal to a committee meeting and then to a discussion with a librettist, putting the whole of his mind from one thing to another without any hesitation. People have often remarked on the speed with which he wrote his music; but he nearly always thought about each work for a long time before beginning to write it. The *Missa brevis*, for example, was written in only a few days, but he had been thinking about it for more than six months. Whenever he was actually writing, his concentration was impregnable: I remember one pouring day when he got soaked through while sitting indoors at his desk because he hadn't noticed that the rain was coming in on him.

I first met him in 1943, and during the next few years did various odd jobs for him. Then, in 1952, when I was already training the Aldeburgh Festival Choir, he asked me to orchestrate *Rejoice in the Lamb* for that year's festival as he hadn't time to do it himself. It was a formidable request. Luckily he approved of my instrumentation, and soon afterwards he suggested that I should come and live in Aldeburgh, to work as his amanuensis and to help in the running of the festival.

That was in September 1952, and he had just begun writing *Gloriana*, which had been commissioned to celebrate the

[1] From the *Musical Times*, 1977.

Coronation in June 1953. Covent Garden wanted the vocal score by the middle of February, so he planned a timetable for getting each act finished. Every morning he wrote from about 8.30 to 12.30; then he took the manuscript to the piano and played through what he had written. He usually went back to work at 4.00 and kept at it until 7.30 or 8.00. His pencil sketches were remarkably clear to read. My job was to write out the vocal score so that it could be reproduced for the singers. He gave me helpful advice about my piano reductions, telling me to add a tremolando in brackets for a gradual crescendo on slow sustained brass chords, and to indicate in small notes above the stave any rapid 'out-of-reach' woodwind passages. He never allowed a convenient pianistic division between the two hands on the keyboard to disguise the clear outlines of the music.

He began the full score of *Gloriana* in February 1953 and we then had to work for at least ten hours a day in order to get through it in a month. I prepared the 34-stave pages for him, spacing the bar lines, writing the clefs and signatures, copying out the vocal lines, and eventually filling in any instruments that were to be doubled. We sat side by side at separate tables, and I was dismayed to see how quickly he wrote – he could get through twenty-eight pages in a day. I thought I should never catch up with him. On one occasion he had reckoned to get to the end of a scene by 4.00, but he finished it just after midday and, as usual, he turned round while he put in the last note, saying, 'Now in the *next* scene. . . .' He seldom had to stop and think. There were a few momentary queries: could trombones glissando a 4th fairly low down? Could the bass clarinet flutter-tongue? What were the shakes that the bassoon couldn't manage? My first chance to keep pace with him was when he reached the tutti contrapuntal entries at 'Green leaves are we, Red rose our golden Queen.' Here, to my great relief, he stopped and thought for nearly three-quarters of an hour, matching the details of the woodwind tonguing or the string bowing with the subtle sound of each final consonant in the words.

He was always patient about my many mistakes. It is true that he could be very angry; but he was fundanentally a calm person. He was often depressed, especially after a bad performance. In a letter he wrote to me in 1948 he said, 'How *essential* good performances are! I have recently heard several performances of my own pieces and I felt so depressed that I considered chucking it all up! Wrong tempi, stupid phrasing and poor technique – in fact nonsense.'

He was frequently weary. I remember once, when he was halfway through a full score, he asked, 'Did your father *always* enjoy working?' And when the vast score of *The Prince of the Pagodas* was at last finished he wrote to me, saying, 'Thank God it is over and done with (all except those . . . metronome marks).' It was the strain of having to live the double life of composer–performer that was the chief cause of his weariness. Foreign orchestral concert tours were particularly exhausting. In a letter he wrote to me from Aldeburgh in 1968 he said:

Just off to Germany – what a life! – how I wish one could sit quietly and just get on with work; but it won't last forever, and one day I'll be able to relax a bit, and try and become a good composer.

Proof-reading often had to be dealt with while he was travelling from one country to the next. When we were writing a book together, called *The Story of Music*, I used to get pages of his criticism sent from abroad:

That old vexed question of nature v. art! ! I suggest that the paragraph should end – 'an artist needs to have courage and imagination, as well as energy and skill, for he has to create something that will have a life of its own, with the vitality of Nature's own creations.' That gets rid of what I don't like, the suggestion of *rivalry* with Nature.

During the years when I was his amanuensis there was always plenty of variety in the unexpected jobs that had to be done. While he was writing *Gloriana* he had been unable to begin Act 2 Scene 3 because he didn't know the steps and figures of a pavane, galliard, volta or coranto. So I took the day off and went and had lessons on how to dance them, in order to teach him what he needed to know before he wrote the appropriate tunes. (He said that I was to swear to tell him directly the music began to 'turn into a pastiche'.) During rehearsals of *The Turn of the Screw* one of my jobs was to teach the thirteen-year-old David

Hemmings to pretend to be playing Miles's piano solo on the bare surface of a table while the actual sound came from the orchestral pianist in the pit: each gesture had to look sufficiently convincing to deceive the audience in the Venice Opera House. In *Noyes Fludde*, Britten had had the idea of hitting teacups with teaspoons to represent the sound of the first raindrops falling on the ark, but he came round to me one afternoon saying that he'd tried it out at teatime and it wouldn't work. By great good fortune I had once had to teach Women's Institute percussion groups during wartime 'social half-hour', so I was able to take him into my kitchen and show him how a row of china mugs hanging on a length of string could be hit with a large wooden spoon. Other unexpected jobs included rehearsing 'the tongs and bones' in *A Midsummer Night's Dream*, and conducting the offstage trumpets in the recording of *The Prince of the Pagodas*. He used to find recording sessions more exhausting than anything else, and dreaded the days when he had to stop writing a new opera in order to record the one before last.

Many other things threatened to interrupt his regular hours of work. There were innumerable letters to be written to all the young musicians who asked for his advice. There were the many friends in distress who had to be helped if possible ('One can't pick up *every* pebble on the beach, because one's hands aren't large enough to hold them.') There were the amateur members of the Aldeburgh Music Club, turning up in a state of terrified ecstasy when he offered to play the viola with them in the Schubert C major quintet. And there was his own conscience, nagging him because of his dislike of the music of certain established composers: every now and then he used to read an unloved score as a bedside book from 11.00 p.m. onwards, taking another look to be quite sure he hadn't been mistaken ('Anyway, I've done Brahms now and needn't get him out again for another three years or so.')

The Aldeburgh Festival, which he cared about so passionately, took up a great deal of his time and energy. In our frequent three-hour discussions about programmes he was quicker and clearer than anyone else. And he was always aware of the difficulties of organizing a festival. Long before Snape

Maltings became available, he knew that we should have to have our own theatre. But there were many problems. In a letter to me from Hong Kong in 1956 he wrote:

> I was a little alarmed by the reticence of [a few of the committee's] approval of the *whole* Theatre project (much doubt being expressed as to whether it's a good idea) and without that can one *really* go ahead and raise money for the site? That's a kind of responsibility that I can't face alone.

The festival may often have seemed a burden to him, but it was an essential part of his working life. Among its many blessings, it helped to teach him how to conduct. Those who first knew him as a great conductor during the 1960s may not have realized that he was trying to get his technique better and better throughout the 1940s and 1950s. At the 1953 Aldeburgh Festival, when he was having trouble with his arm as a result of writing too many pages every day, he said, 'I'll have to learn a different way of conducting if I'm to get through this weekend; I suppose it's because I'm too tense nearly all the time.' Six months later he was saying that he would have to learn to conduct with very small movements, and that it would be a lesson in control, which was what he felt he needed more and more.

In 1964 I had to give up working as his amanuensis because of the increasing demands for performances and recordings of my father's music. I went on working for the Aldeburgh Festival, and there were occasional writing jobs for Britten, such as helping him to edit a concert version of Purcell's *The Fairy Queen*. This was an enthralling task which I enjoyed as much as any of the things he has ever asked me to do for him. I have often wished that I had written down what he said about the technical problems we were trying to solve.

When I first began working for him in 1952 I kept a diary, but soon had to give it up because there was never time to spare. On re-reading it, I have been reminded of several of his characteristic remarks. For instance, on the day when the 'Commentary on his works from a group of specialists' was published, he said, 'I've come to the conclusion that I must have a very clever subconscious.' Then once, after a depressing committee meeting, he said that he wanted in future to be able to 'think more and more about less and less'. And on my first evening in Aldeburgh the entry in my diary says:

We were talking about old age and he said that he had a very strong feeling that people died at the right moment, and that the greatness of a person included the time when he was born and the time he endured, but that this was difficult to understand.

*

So wrote Imogen Holst in the *Musical Times* shortly after Britten's death. Much of the planning for each year's festival, while she was concerned with it, was done on Boxing Day. Britten never conceived programmes for any other reason than that he loved the music concerned. When it came to the works themselves he took endless trouble to make sure the right edition was being used. He was a prime enemy of ill-marked copies and bad editing. Miss Holst recalls rubbing out acres of pencil marks on hired copies and remembers, as she puts it, 'living on a carpet of india-rubber crumbs'.

He was always aware of every detail of scoring in a work, and also of the extreme economy needed to make the festival a success. If he could do without a third trumpet here, or a second bassoon there, he would make it possible. When Miss Holst began working for him in the autumn of 1952, it was a revelation for her to see just how practical he was. The only comparable person in that respect was her father.

Britten took great care to get the order of pieces within a programme right, and also the order of events in the whole festival. Balance was of the essence. There must be variety, and the important events should be carefully spaced.

She found the strain of working at his compositions was considerable. She would often start work at his house at 8.30 in the morning and leave at 10.30 at night. But she found it a marvellous experience that was thoroughly worthwhile. Britten was a hard taskmaster, and the job of making piano reductions sometimes seemed impossible. What was one to do, for instance, with the beginning of the *Nocturne*, where the texture and counterpoint depended so much on instrumental colouring, and where the different keys needed a 'mixed' notation? It took three attempts on Miss Holst's part to satisfy the composer. In such cases he was infinitely patient.

His rehearsals were amazing. Miss Holst has observed conductors at work since the age of five when she was taken by her father to a rehearsal by Sir Henry Wood of one of Holst's works. Since then, she has grown sceptical about some conductors' gestures and about their habit of shouting and bullying. Other conductors have been too easy-going. Her father was kindly but firm and never wasted a moment of time. There was strictness but with courtesy behind it. It was the same with Britten. He never lost his temper, except when there was any sign of slackness. With amateurs he was very encouraging, and he used to play the viola part in the Schubert C major quintet with members of the Aldeburgh Music Club.

Miss Holst has said that, during their many walks together, their discussions were nearly always about music, and were very often concerned with the work he was then writing. *Noyes Fludde* was planned on such a walk. He would also talk more generally about music, often being critical of the avant-garde. The lack of a tune and lack of any feeling of tonality worried him considerably. He thought there were many years of life left for music founded on tonality. It was on his solitary walks that he used to struggle to find the way out of a composing difficulty. If he was dissatisfied with one of his ideas, he would go over and over it again in search of a solution. On the rare occasions when he became stuck, he used to feel desperately depressed.

While she was working for him, Miss Holst would always speak her mind, trying to be as helpful as possible. Once, when she was copying out one of the dances in *Gloriana*, his sketch had a cadence that worried her as being too weak, so she mentioned it to him. He seemed a little taken aback, but went away to think about it. A few days later, he told her that she had been right and that he had altered the chord. In revising his scores after a first performance he would often make slight alterations. He always insisted on these revisions before a work was published.

*

Above: Benjamin Britten aged approximately five years with family and friends. *Seated left to right:* Britten's father, his mother, Liza Suter Schlotterbech, and (seated on the ground) Winifred Rix, Britten and sister Beth

Right: Joan Cross, with Britten at Schipol airport during the 1951 English Opera Group Tour of Holland

An English Opera Group concert introduced by the Earl of Harewood. *Left to right:* Rowland Jones, Nancy Evans, Lord Harewood, Joan Cross, Michael Langdon, and Britten at the piano

The Amadeus Quartet and Britten at the Aldeburgh Festival, 1952; Marion Thorpe (then Lady Harewood) is turning the pages

Basil Coleman and Joan Cross rehearsing for *Gloriana* with Britten at Orme Square, 1953

A programme planning session between Imogen Holst, Benjamin Britten and Peter Pears

Above: Myfanwy Piper with Britten at a rehearsal for *A Midsummer Night's Dream*, Aldeburgh 1960

Left: Tippett and Britten at a party to celebrate Tippett's sixtieth birthday

Britten was not a teacher – he said so himself – but throughout his working life, at every rehearsal he took, his players and singers learnt from him. As long ago as 1953, when Miss Holst had just begun working at Aldeburgh for Britten, he said to her, 'What you and Peter and I have got to remember is that we're going to have a music school here one day.' The music school that he had hoped then for was born at the Maltings in 1973 with a weekend for singers directed by Pears. Britten was by then an invalid, but during the next three years he was always ready with criticism and encouragement, and the Britten–Pears School of Advanced Musical Studies has become his memorial.

*

Quotations from letters by BB to Imogen Holst and from her diary of 1952-54

Letter of 28 July 1949 (after first performance of the Spring Symphony *on 9 July in Amsterdam):*

It is worth going through all the agonies of writing when there is someone. . . who sees what one is after. . . . There must be a balance between instinct and intelligence – either without the other is useless but how rare is the combination!

Diary of 19 December 1952 (re last act of Gloriana):

He said that it was the octave E natural which had given him the idea of the Coda – he hadn't had a notion of what to do, and then when he *heard* the E natural he knew the first bit had got to come back again.

Diary of 30 July 1953

He said there was a test of listening in the storm in the *Grimes* Interlude – one instrument was playing a fifth too low, and he couldn't discover which it was: it was the first time he had ever been defeated by such a thing.

Diary of 28 January 1954 (re orchestral rehearsals of Gloriana *at Covent Garden):*

He said, 'The rehearsal was *infinitely* better than the day before.' He asked me to stay on to talk about the possibilities of an Aldeburgh theatre. It was extraordinary to see how, as usual, he could put the whole of his mind from one thing to another, like lightning.

9

Sir Michael Tippett

First Encounters

I first met Benjamin Britten during the war, when I was musical director at Morley College. We wanted a tenor soloist for Gibbons's verse anthem *My Beloved Spake*. Walter Bergmann, who was then chorus master in Morley, suggested Peter Pears, recently returned from America. When Pears came to rehearsal, Britten came with him. I can recall the occasion very clearly.

I had in fact seen Britten before the war at the first public performance of *A Boy was Born* at a Lemare concert in the old Mercury Theatre, Notting Hill.[1] I had no intuition then that the slim figure walking down the gangway to take his bow before the public would become so decisive and beloved a personality in my life. But I have an unusually vivid mental picture of that moment. The aural memory is much vaguer. It is really only of the Brosa Quartet madly counting quavers in the finale of my first quartet, also a premiere!

Though Britten and I met over one of the Elizabethans, our real musical connection was Purcell. It is a rough generalisation, but there is some truth in the contention that while a 30 to 40-year older figure like Vaughan Williams derived special emotional and musical sustenance from the Elizabethans (cf. the *Tallis Fantasia, Sir John in Love*). Britten and I submitted to the influence of Purcell to a degree not seen in English music before. I won't recount what are the points of Purcell we chiefly needed, but certainly we responded to the carry and freedom

[1] 17 December 1934. The first performance had been a BBC broadcast in April the same year.

of his vocal line.

It was also during the war, and not long after I first met Britten, that I was asked by the then Precentor of Canterbury Cathedral to hear one of his lay-clerks sing. This was Alfred Deller. He sang Purcell's *Music for a While*. One outcome of this meeting and of the growing friendship with Peter Pears was the first full-scale performance by Morley College of Purcell's *1692 Ode for St Cecilia's Day*, with the ravishing duet for counter-tenor and tenor in that work sung by those two incomparable artists accompanied by a bevy of recorders.[2] I don't remember if Britten was present, but I am pretty sure he was.

About this time I wrote my first piece of music for Pears and Britten as a duo. Out of the study of Purcell and Monteverdi had come the urge to write a vocal cantata (as opposed to a song cycle). This piece was *Boyhood's End* and the first performance was given by them in the Holst Room at Morley College.[3]

Ben later asked me what larger works I had written, if any, other than those he knew. I told him of *A Child of Our Time*, of how I had played it to Walter Goehr some time before, who advised me in the circumstances to shut it up in a drawer, which, being rather patient and literal, I had. Ben had the manuscript out of the drawer at once. In looking through the score he noticed how, in one of the Spirituals, the effect could be greatly enhanced by lifting the tenor solo part suddenly an octave higher. This I entirely agreed with and so this minute piece of Britten composition is in the score. He persuaded us to venture on a performance; he was already then close to the Sadler's Wells Opera and persuaded three of their singers to sing for us: Joan Cross, Peter Pears and Roderick Lloyd. The fourth, Margaret McArthur, came from us at Morley. In the event, through no fault of these artists, it was an imperfect premiere[4] under execrable conditions, but inescapably moving. One year later, Britten's own relations with Sadler's Wells bore

[2] 31 December 1944, at Friends House, Euston Road.

[3] 5 June 1943.

[4] 19 March 1944 at the Adelphi Theatre.

fruit, with the premiere of *Peter Grimes*.[5]

Ben and I met first in the war, when we were both conscientious objectors. Here is a small anecdote of those times. It is customary for artists to give concerts free to inmates of HM prisons. Britten and Pears had already offered to do so before I was sent to prison myself. They managed to arrange it that they gave a recital in Wormwood Scrubs when I was there.[6] On my side I am ashamed to mention the untruthful wangling by which I convinced the authorities that the recital was impossible unless I turned the pages for the pianist. To the last moment it was touch and go. But finally I stepped out of the ranks and sat down on the platform beside him. A strange moment for us both. He remembers, I am sure, that 'primitive responsive audience' of gaol-birds. It is exactly twenty years ago. But these twenty years have piled up the works in that catalogue, right up to the *War Requiem* where his pacifism, as much else, has found decisive utterance.

Britten at 50[7]

I will begin with an objective fact. Britten's publishers[8] are producing a catalogue of all his work to date – to his 50th year that is. There are 99 published works as separate items in this catalogue. Ten of these are operas; seven of them are major vocal works for the concert hall; four are large-scale orchestral works; there are three canticles, two string quartets, not to speak of works for small choirs (a favourite of mine is the *Hymn to St Cecilia*), small groups of all kinds, music for all occasions.

Considering the artistically chaotic period in which we live, without an agreed musical style, so that composers must wrestle with their own language in a manner unknown say to Mozart, and considering the tremendous range of subjects, in the widest sense of the word, which Britten has involved himself in, then

[5] 7 June 1945.

[6] 11 July 1943.

[7] First published in the *Observer*, 17 November 1963.

[8] Boosey and Hawkes.

the sheer scale of his accomplishment is staggering. Here is the first of the facets of his genius. Phenomenal productivity arising from the combination of great gifts with continuous hard work.

Britten's technical mastery is often treated as part of the musical gifts which mother nature undoubtedly showered on him. But this mastery was not a gift at all (like the ability in childhood to win chess tournaments from older masters). It is the result of sheer hard work. If anyone can be said to have been initially responsible for his temper in the critical early years, then it was Frank Bridge. But once that has been said it still needs to be realized that the hard work is done year in year out by Britten himself. By hard work I am not thinking so much of the hours of intense activity, but rather of the prolonged struggle, even agony, which composition is for Britten. In a letter to me he writes:

> I am having a ferocious time between these public functions and my own work (more and more difficult!) but that's our old problem, isn't it?

By 'our', he meant that I (who better being so close a colleague?) would immediately understand this problem of creative work as against public presentation. But he also meant by 'problem' the unending struggle within the work of composition itself. And 'more and more difficult!' means just what it says. The older we grow in art and the profounder our sensibilities, the more we find creation – despite all the mastery of experience – difficult.

We can uncover now a further facet of his genius. For if we consider the difficulties, not of the future for him, but simply of the past, we can see that Britten by his very gifts had his full share of the problems bequeathed to us all in this period. There being no single tradition now, each artist forges his links (or blows up his bridges) according solely to temperament for his individual *kairos*. Britten's *kairos* has never been, even in extreme youth (nor will be in the future), to make his music out of destruction. (I use the word destruction in its healthy, affirmative sense.) It is interesting that Britten said of his youthful admiration of Auden, 'Auden was a powerful revolutionary figure. He was very much anti-bourgeois and that appealed.' Yet there is no early Britten work to match Auden's 'The Orators' for example. Britten must make his music out of his own creative gifts in relation *always* to the music of our forebears. So that he is inescapably involved in a fiendish problem of choice. That is, for each work he has to choose (in his finest works only after agonising struggles) the style and substance afresh and in relation to some tradition. For the purposes of his own music, in nearly every work, his intuitions in this respect were infallible.

As a third facet of his genius I treasure his lucidity. As Britten said to Murray Schafer 'Music for me is clarification; I try to clarify, to refine, to sensitise. Stravinsky once said that one must work perpetually at one's technique. But what is technique? Schoenberg's technique is often a tremendous elaboration. My technique is to tear all the waste away; to achieve perfect clarity of expression, that is my aim.'[9]

Britten does not misunderstand Stravinsky nor criticize Schoenberg. He points a finger to himself, because *that* is what he had to be.

Turning now to his productions there is nothing useful in parading here my likes or dislikes. Nor shall I make any judgement of quality with regard to his works. I am a composer (and a deeply attached friend) not a critic. There is also a further reason, which I will discuss in a moment. What I have to say concerns style and individual voice. Britten, as everyone knows who listens much to his music, has a marked style of his own. We can always immediately recognize any 'piece of music' by him, and can trace imitations of this style in younger admirers. But every composer with enough personality to possess an individual voice writes works which go further. Of these works we tend to say not merely that this is by so-and-so, but that this is such-and-such a work. (Think of *Tristan and Isolde* – then think of *Meistersinger*.) So, however much Britten grew beyond *Peter Grimes*, there are tones, procedures, orchestral and vocal colours which are more than just Britten in his general style, for

[9] Murray Schafer *British Composers in Interview* (London, 1963).

they have such a 'Grimes'-ness about them, they are that opera; and none other.

For me, though this has not been recognized so generally, the style of the *Spring Symphony* has also this quality. A gaiety and exuberance unique and inimitable. Between these poles of dark and light (*Grimes* and the *Spring Symphony*), is the style of the Canticles; flower of his natural piety. We are both of us religious composers, i.e. bound, *religati*, to a sense of the numinous, but Britten is more properly Christian.

To attempt an account of Britten's place in contemporary music is to enter on a vexed question, bedevilled by the inability of so many music critics and others to distinguish between the facts of public acclaim and the pretentions (and maybe necessity) of value judgements. To deal with the facts first. When his own generation comes into the title, that is, when the substantial figures of Stravinsky and Hindemith reside in the memory, then Britten will share the top of the world's acclaim solely with Shostakovich. This is an honour for England (and of course for Russia) and we may 'shine forth' through Britten as a country of no mean musical worth. We want more of this not less. That is, the world audience for music, and the huge audiences that are to come, can explore and enjoy more such figures. To assess Britten's music in a judgement of value is to my mind pretention not fact. It will only be a fact when his works are *all* there (we have as yet not the half) and he too must reside in the memory. Yet I am in no way suggesting that critics should not make value judgements of new music, Britten's or anyone's. That is the burden of their job. We need, I think, more judgements, illuminatory assessments of the general stage of musical affairs; especially, one would think of the state of the emperor's clothes. But not on the other hand a manic hunt for masterpieces and the one true way announced of God. This is stultifying, expecially to the younger English composers struggling to find their individual song. (I make this plea within the birthday tribute to an older figure, because Britten himself would so signally approve my saying so.)

Great disservice has been done to Britten by the indiscriminate coupling of his name with great figures of the past. It cannot be too clearly stated that this can never have emanated from the composer himself. He does not ask himself, 'Am I the xxxxxxxx of my time?' But: 'How can I hammer out these objective works of art which are the proper and full fruits of my gifts in relation to this period?'

Obituary[10]

The news of Benjamin Britten's death brought a sense of loss to every musical person of the whole world. To those like myself who knew him closely, the sense of loss is probably no greater. I have memories that go back for a very long period. But I think of him now, in 1945, just after the war, when he had come back from America to England, and I remember walking into the darkened auditorium of Sadler's Wells Opera Theatre, and there was a high sound of violins – in fact, the very opening of the first interlude of *Peter Grimes* – and, with his back to me, this shadowy figure in the orchestral pit, rehearsing the orchestra. And I remember remarking to myself at that time how fantastically professional this young man was who had not only composed this work, but was performing it there with all the authority of a top-ranking conductor. It is difficult for us now, after so many years, to realize what this event, in every sense, meant, not only to us in England but to, I think, the musical world in general. Because, though it did, in fact, happen first in England, the resonances were, in the end, and very quickly indeed, international. But, in England itself, the sense of excitement was probably due to the feeling that here, at last, after the very first performance on the stage, was an opera whose professionalism, whose quality, in the best sense of the word, was something which had not been seen in England since the single completed opera, *Dido and Aeneas*, of Henry Purcell, centuries before.

For Britten himself, this triumph meant something more than the immediacy of being an internationally recognised

[10] Published in the *Listener*, 16 December 1976.

composer. It meant for him that he was now willing in himself, and, indeed, determined to be, within the 20th century, a professional opera composer. That in itself is an extraordinarily difficult thing to do, and one of the achievements for which he will always be remembered in musical history books, is that, in fact, he actually *did* it. For himself, this meant that he had to consider very seriously the question of the economics of opera in modern society, or rather the society of that time, 1945, just after the war, when as far as England was concerned, it was a period of impoverishment. He considered the matter in great detail and at length with Peter Pears, the singer, and between them they decided that it was possible to have operas of quality and power using a very much smaller number of players in the orchestral pit.

In order to do this, the two of them decided they should found the English Opera Group, a small group of professional singers who were, in general, to be accompanied by a brilliant group of up to twelve instrumental players. In order that the English Opera Group should have a permanent place where it could perform the operas written for it, Peter Pears and Benjamin Britten decided that they would begin a festival in Aldeburgh where they lived, and, though conditions seemed improbable, it is true that within a very tiny building in that old town, this whole series of Britten works was conceived and produced. Indeed, this series contained, for me at least, one masterpiece that equals *Grimes* in the larger opera house, and that is *The Turn of the Screw*, to the libretto out of Henry James.

Nearly as fascinating as the whole series of opera, to my mind, is the whole series of song cycles. These were written, generally, for Peter Pears, the tenor, and one must realize that this close and intimate relationship produced from Britten some of the most tender, beautiful music that he ever wrote. I first heard them sung during the war at a very early, if not the first, performance of the *Michelangelo Sonnets*, and I can remember again, as a composer, being struck by this extraordinary musicality of composition, of performance, with an additional sense of surprise, indeed, almost bewilderment, that they were written to Italian words, with such a fantastic sense, so far as I could hear, of the relation of the music to the Italian. So it is really no surprise that, within this series of works for voice and piano, or voice and small numbers of instruments also, Britten wrote music not only in English, but in French, in German, and even, indeed, in Russian.

I would also say that this seems to me the way in which we should appreciate this composer, as being a figure who lived nearly all his life totally within his native country, but who always had a professional and international attitude to the music of his time. And surely we can see that his pacifism and his feelings about international war sprang from something of the same source, and that, sooner or later, this passion concerning the things that human beings did to each other during the two great wars that he had lived through would issue in some profound work of art. I am referring, of course, to the *War Requiem* which he meditated on many years before it was actually performed.

I want to say here, personally, that Britten has been for me the most purely musical person I have ever met and I have ever known. It always seemed to me that music sprang out of his fingers when he played the piano, as it did out of his mind when he composed. I am sure that the core and centre of his great achievements lies in the works for voices and instruments.

Through his extraordinary musicality and fantastic technical equipment, Britten was probably one of the finest accompanists on the piano of anyone of his generation. Anybody who heard Pears and Britten, year after year, do their annual recital at the Aldeburgh Festival or, luckily, heard them during the great tours they took right round the world, has a memory which, I feel, is ineffaceable. But I think that all of us who were close to Ben had for him something dangerously near to love. And it gave us, perhaps, an anguished sensibility for what might happen to this figure.

It seems to me that certain obsessions belonged naturally to the works of art which he produced. I don't think it matters at all that they may not in any way have belonged to his personality. I refer to a deep sense of cruelty, cruelty upon people, cruelty as a suffering. A sense, I think, also of the fragility of all existence, leading him to a sense of death. He had a special sensitivity, I am sure, for the works of Henry James, and the whole period running from 1890 to 1910, during which a figure like Thomas Mann was writing. The penultimate opera, *Owen Wingrave*, had been in Britten's mind as an intended opera years and years ago, probably even before he returned to England from America. In *Wingrave*, the artistic obsession with cruelty and death is clear for us to see, but a sense of death was sharper still in *Death in Venice*, the last of all operas. Here is a work of extraordinary tenderness, and I think all the love which he had for his singer flowed out into this work. But there was a sense, with those of us outside the immediate circle, of apprehension: an apprehension which was deepened as we knew of his illness. The apprehension is totally fulfilled, and we are left with a sense of sorrow and loss.

10

Joan Cross

During the early forties, when Peter Pears was engaged to sing with the wartime Sadler's Wells Opera, Britten was noticed in the audience of performances of Mozart and Rossini in which Pears was involved. The word soon got round that he was engaged in writing an opera – a matter, needless to say, of consuming interest. He was shortly after persuaded to play some of his score to the directors and the staff of the company; the impression it made was immediate and startling.

There was talk of the end of the war and the re-opening of the Sadler's Wells Theatre.[1] Not unnaturally, this new opera seemed almost ideal for the occasion of the return to Rosebery Avenue, if it could be arranged. Britten was in favour and eventually the publishers agreed.

It was not, however, plain sailing. Rehearsals revealed that the company found the story and music antipathetic. The music staff reported it hard on the voices and said they found the new idiom strange and unacceptable.

The company, at the end of an exhausting tour in wartime conditions, and singing a limited repertory, would have found it vastly preferable to re-open Sadler's Wells with an established favourite such as *Carmen* or *Trovatore*. Then the principal singers could have renewed acquaintance with their prewar successes. Instead they found themselves cast in what seemed to them to be *minor* roles. Finally, they had no faith in the piece. All of this made for an atmosphere of extreme disharmony.

'"Good luck! Whatever happens we were right to do this piece," was Tyrone Guthrie's[2] not over-enthusiastic encour-

[1] Closed from 1940 to 1945.

[2] Sir Tyrone Guthrie – then general administrator of Sadler's Wells and the Old Vic.

agement to me just before the curtain went up on the first night; he reflected the doubts and anxieties current in the company. The overwhelming success of that first night is now operatic history.

'I shared, to a certain extent this nervousness in performing in the new idiom. Bred as I was on *Traviata* and *Bohéme*, I found it hard to memorize and technically hard to accomplish (the embroidery aria is as testing as Pamina's G minor aria in *The Magic Flute* or the last-act *scena* of Verdi's *Otello*).

What gives lasting pleasure in performing Britten's operas is his unfailing sense of theatre. He has an exact picture in his mind of what's supposed to be happening on stage and gives his discerning performer the exact amount of time in which to do it.'

The uncomfortable experiences during the presentation of *Peter Grimes* at Sadler's Wells made Britten think that he would be happier writing on a more intimate scale for a smaller and more sympathetic group of singers and players. With his youthful, eager vision and with the support of Pears, Eric Crozier[3] and others, the English Opera Group came into being and a new operatic enterprise was launched.

The Rape of Lucretia and *Albert Herring* were written at considerable speed for the new company, the last pages being handed over to the cast of *Lucretia* at a very late stage of rehearsal.

At about this time, the operatic concerts devised by Lord Harewood (q.v.) were taking place. Peter Pears, Nancy Evans and Owen Brannigan were among the other singers. It was an extraordinary experience to perform these operatic excerpts with Britten at the piano because he was able to suggest the full orchestra in his playing. Joan Cross particularly recalls a scene from *Pelléas* with herself as Mélisande and Pears as Pelléas, and another from Ravel's *L'Heure Espagnoe*. Similarly, Britten was a great inspiration when he directed his own operas: *Herring* became inspired when he conducted it because of his great sense of humour and his energy. When he played a chord at the start of Lady Billow's address in the party scene, he would convulse the audience as nobody else did, even before Joan Cross began to sing.

After *Billy Budd*, Britten wrote *Gloriana* with Joan Cross in

[3] Producer of the first performance of *Peter Grimes*.

mind as Elizabeth I. Vocally and dramatically, it was a strong challenge to her at that stage in her career. She feels that she did it greater justice as an actress than as a singer, but those who saw and heard her in the part would find it hard to divorce one part of the interpretation from the other, so gloriously – right word – did she fit the role. Again there were resentments, which sprang from envy that Britten rather than an older colleague had been given the Coronation commission. Joan remembers that, at the premiere, the hostility of the establishment audience was almost tangible on stage. The notices were unfavourable and the piece seemed a failure until it returned to the repertory the following autumn, when it was highly acclaimed.

Joan Cross undertook the part of Mrs Grose in the performances of *The Turn of the Screw* against her better judgement. It was the first time she had been invited to sing a comprimario role and she cared little for it. To please Britten, she sang it but was never convinced that she did the part full justice or, finally, pleased the composer – not that he showed displeasure. On the contrary, he was always deeply grateful to the artists who performed his work, even, it seemed, when they did not *excel.* When he got what he expected from a singer, his appreciation was gratifying.

'Over the ten years during which I sang for Britten – I was concerned with five premieres – he was never less than a stimulating, understanding and warmhearted colleague. He was wonderfully appreciative of any effort made on his behalf by his artists and never failed to express his pleasure in a good performance. When, as sometimes inevitably happened, something went wrong, he was quite unable to express his displeasure and took refuge in silence, which was disconerting.

'Age blurs memory; hindsight tells me that I had a special relationship with Britten which arose out of my contribution as a performer in his operas. But I could not claim a *close friendship.* I think he chose few close friends; his intimate association with Pears satisfied his needs musically, intellectually and emotionally. I retain a lasting memory of a man of great charm and a glorious sense of humour, given to occasional and sudden bursts of fury (which he often regretted later) and of course total dedication.'

11
Sir Frederick Ashton

When Sir Frederick Ashton first met Britten, shortly before the war, in the company of William Walton, who already had the greatest admiration for Britten as a composer, he had the feeling that he was in the presence of a genius because of Britten's extraordinary eyes. After the war, Ashton choreographed the Frank Bridge *Variations*, with the consent of the composer, and then, in the United States, *Les Illuminations* – a rather fantastic version of Rimbaud's life.

Then came *Albert Herring* at Glyndebourne in 1947, the first production by the newly formed English Opera Group. That staging by Ashton was always considered definitive by the composer, but it was not born without many labour pains. The causes were twofold: the opposition of John Christie, or at least his dislike of the music, and the dissatisfaction of Eric Crozier, the librettist, with Ashton's somewhat burlesque approach to the characters. Ashton recalls that he made them all slightly ludicrous, and Crozier believed that they should be played 'straight'. Ashton still believes his approach was the right one, because the people depicted in Britten's score are comical. At one point Ashton was prepared to withdraw from the production, but when the cast had wind of his intended resignation they protested and declared that they would not continue unless he remained.

Ashton was not aware of what Christie's feud with Britten was about. All he knew was that Britten, who was conducting, would not let Christie anywhere near anybody concerned with the production. Once in a while Ashton would slip Christie into the auditorium so that he could see what was going on. So fraught was the situation that nobody actually stayed at Glyndebourne; they were whisked off in a bus to their digs, and the only person they were allowed to talk to was Kathleen Ferrier, who was singing Orpheus at the same time.

Already at this stage of his career, Britten was extremely sensitive to criticism and he would not talk to the press. Ashton told him to try to be above that kind of thing, but it was not in Britten's nature. Nevertheless, Ashton recalls the happiness of the team, the fun of Joan Cross in particular as Lady Billows, and the absence of rancour in the cast. On the whole he remembers that the reception was favourable. On Glyndebourne's side the contretemps arose (as Spike Hughes reports in his history of the house) from, what they considered, the lack of gratitude of the English Opera Group to Glyndebourne and the envy of the grant that the company received.

After *Herring*, Ashton made a ballet on the *Young Person's Guide to the Orchestra* for Covent Garden and he was somewhat upset that he had not been asked to do the choreography of the full-length ballet for Covent Garden *The Prince of the Pagodas*, which was choreographed by John Cranko. In any case, he does not feel that the story works very well, because of the hotchpotch of fairy tales, which make it too complicated, although he admires the score.

His next cooperation with the composer was on *Death in Venice*, in which Ashton did the choreography for the dancing. There were difficulties. The children used hardly had the necessary strength, particularly as the whole 'Games of Apollo' sequence is very long – too long in Ashton's opinion. He urged Britten to shorten it, but all the composer was willing to do was snip out a bar or two here and there. However, he did persuade Britten to take the Mother out of the ballet. On the other hand, Britten was willing and able to take Ashton's advice on the devising of the sequence, and they worked together quite closely on it. 'It was a great pleasure to be collaborating with him; I greatly admired him.'

As an artist, Britten had a tremendous passion and dedication in all he did, but he had no great experience of the difficulties involved in writing ballet music. He generally expected Ashton to adapt his dances to the music after it had been written, although there were many discussions about the matter at the Red House and at Britten's cottage at Horham. Ashton feels that Britten was courting him to do the choreography for *Death in Venice*, so he was prepared to listen to what Ashton, with his immense experience in his own field, had to say about working out the Games – even if Britten was unwilling to foreshorten his music: every bar seemed to be sacred.

When working on *Death in Venice* at Aldeburgh, Ashton found that Britten had an almost godlike aura; he was placed on a pinnacle above everyone else. 'I am not sure if that was a good thing for a creative artist. Coming from the rough-and-tumble of Covent Garden where nobody has respect for anyone, I found this almost holy aura a little hard to take. In any case, that hero-worshipping contrasted with the down-to-earth practicality of the composer himself when at work; he was a true man of the theatre.'

12
Lord Harewood

Lord Harewood vividly recalls the first occasion on which he really became aware of Britten as a composer – it was in 1942 when he was in the army. He had been newly commissioned, and was on guard duty. Although 'captive', that is in one place, for twenty-four hours, he and the other soldiers were allowed to send a drummer boy, a young musician of about eighteen, to purchase anything they liked – usually food and drink. In Harewood's case the request was for records. He had just read in the *Gramophone* magazine a review of Britten's *Michelangelo Sonnets* recorded by Pears and the composer on one plum-label 12-inch and one 10-inch 78. He played the records several times, and was captivated by the music, he was attracted by its dramatic quality. Harewood believes that he must have previously heard the Frank Bridge *Variations* at some stage, but he did not know those well. Enthusiastic about every work he encountered after that, Harewood has been continually sympathetic to Britten's way of expressing himself musically. His was a non-insular reaction to the kind of insularity then prevalent in English music.

Some months later, he met the composer for the first time, at a performance by the Sadler's Wells Company, at the New Theatre, with Peter Pears as a principal tenor. The work was *La Traviata*, with Peter Pears as Alfredo. Joan Cross introduced Britten to Harewood, who was immediately impressed by the composer, although they did not really get to know each other until somewhat later, as Lord Harewood's military duties soon took him abroad, and he became a prisoner of war. As soon as the war was over, he began avidly acquiring what records were available of Britten's compositions and attending performances of his music – at that time, these were far less frequent, particularly on the radio, than they were to be later.

Harewood attended the now-legendary first night of *Peter Grimes* in 1945 (and indeed most premieres of Britten's work thereafter, right up to *Death in Venice*). The effect on that first audience was, in Harewood's word, 'monumental' because it was the first genuinely successful British opera, Gilbert and Sullivan apart, since *Dido and Aeneas*. It surpassed everyone's expectations. Harewood recalls that in the foyer beforehand, William Walton was somewhat sceptical simply because of the enormity of the effort required to bring off a large-scale opera. All those who with caution hoped for a masterpiece had their hopes fulfilled. The sheer impact of the sound in Sadler's Wells Theatre was electrifying, particularly in the choral cries of 'Peter Grimes!' from downstage. What amazed Harewood and many others was to find a modern composer writing music that was unashamedly melodic with a grateful vocal line, as well as being important and expressive, and a vehicle of so much of his thought. When Harewood heard the earlier *Paul Bunyan*, performed at Snape in the 1970s, he and Edmund Tracey (an English National Opera director) realized that in many ways it was more advanced, in its operatic solutions, its stylization and musical shortcuts (no didactic explanations of a story), than *Peter Grimes*. But the failure of the earlier piece had convinced Britten to take another way, so that *Grimes* for all its brilliance of invention and dramatic coups, is less ambitious; it is more straightforward in its storytelling and breaks less new ground than *Bunyan*.

In general, Harewood believes, Britten knew precisely what he could do in terms of shaping his music and what he was going to put in those shapes. He had exact aims in front of him but, though he had great inner confidence, he had an outer diffidence, like most creative artists; he respected his public's opinion and might revise his views in the light of it. Harewood considers that he tried to carry out experiments within traditional forms in his succeeding operas. In some ways *The Rape of Lucretia*, which he revised more than his other works, was the most experimental of the operas. *Gloriana* was, in many respects, the most traditional, but even there one finds experiments in the short pieces within it that make big statements. There are traditional operatic statements even in the apparently experimental and stylized *Church Parables*. Part of their greatness is that in each work there is something that speaks to the listener sharply, strongly, individually, and beautifully.

Harewood finds *Billy Budd* probably Britten's most ambitious opera, not technically but emotionally, and he likens it to the position held by *Don Carlos* in Verdi's oeuvre. For a particular pleasure not often found elsewhere in opera, he would choose *A Midsummer Night's Dream*. It is a mounting pleasure – after the exposition of Act 1, the following acts are wonderfully moving in a very special way. In *The Turn of the Screw* Britten achieved the perfection of form he was seeking in his chamber operas; for the Venice Festival of 1954 he was asked to write a piece for his English Opera Group, and he sought and found a work that would precisely satisfy the demands of the moment. When he was asked to write a work for the Coronation the previous year, he very carefully analysed what was wanted. This was discussed by Harewood and Britten on a ski-ing holiday in February 1952, just after the death of George VI. Britten wanted to write a celebratory piece that would sum up, in romantic terms, the burgeoning of a new era, as the Italians and Germans had done in their own particular ways – Verdi in *Aida*, for instance, Weber in *Freischütz* – with operas that express national characteristics. It seemed that the reign of Elizabeth I was the ideal setting for such a work. The subject of Elizabeth and Essex, based on Lytton Strachey's text, was decided upon. That was Britten's brief and, as in nearly every other opera, he fulfilled it magnificently. Harewood thinks that *Owen Wingrave*, a technically most advanced work, was one in which he did not hit his target with complete success. Yet there is one ensemble in *Wingrave* which, in less than a minute, sums up and changes a situation. Perhaps the subject here was almost too easy for him, because from the start all our sympathies must be with Wingrave, whereas in, for instance, *Grimes* and *Budd* our sympathies are subtly divided. Harewood recalls that, when *Grimes* first came out, it was criticized for its lack of a real hero – there was nobody to identify with; but later people, at least the younger ones, realized that to be truthful, a central character must have faults. Harewood thinks that, perhaps subconsciously, Britten was discussing in a parable his own homosexuality. This would have been indicative of his struggle to be accepted – something that everyone who is trying to say something new must go through.

Harewood views *Death in Venice*, which was composed when Britten was seriously ill, as a summing-up of previous achievements. By the time it was written, Britten was less concerned or self-conscious about what others thought of his private life. He knew that they had perhaps accepted it. The work itself is highly praised by Lord Harewood, who finds it compelling – even the long ballet sequence at the end of Act 1, though this was not wholly successful as originally staged. Harewood thinks it is too long but, after listening to it again and again, he finds it completely convincing in its spare, evocative way. The work was the apex of Britten's third period.

Harewood is a firm believer in the shape of a creative artist's life. There is a youthful period; a secure, confident middle period; and a late, visionary period. He cites the painter Turner as an example of what he means, and also Verdi, who had refined and perfected his manner by his last period. This is nature's compensation for older age: greater technical control and enhanced spirituality replace sheer exuberance in creative power. That, he believes, is illustrated in *Death in Venice*: with superior knowledge comes some lessening of invention.

Harewood was at one time a close mentor of the composer. From soon after the first performance of *Grimes* at Covent Garden in 1947 right through the fifties, he saw him a great deal. He had the singular experience of hearing the operas on the piano as they were written, almost week by week. There were many discussions of the music, but Harewood would not go as far as to say he had any influence on it, although there is no doubt that it was Harewood's advocacy that caused *Gloriana* to be performed at the Royal Opera House. Not that, he says, the work was at first a success. He recalls such comments as. 'An insult to a young Queen,' and 'I would rather spend a night in a boiler factory than experience *Gloriana* again.' How curious to find such an open, melodious work so insulted! Harewood believes it was Britten's achievement to be able to treat such a grand historical subject in such movingly human terms.

As a parenthesis, Harewood recalled the attitude of Joan Sutherland to Penelope Rich, a role she took over from Jennifer Vyvyan. Harewood joined the staff of Covent Garden a few days after the premiere of *Gloriana* and, encountering Sutherland back-stage, he discovered that she was hating the thought of taking the part. Some days later she had quite changed her mind. Having studied it closely, she said she had been quite wrong; she now found the part marvellous – and Harewood remembers that she was wonderful in it. That was indicative of prejudice being overcome.

He had long discussions with Britten over his next opera, *The Turn of the Screw*. Having been captivated by the story, Harewood was adamant on the ambivalence of the governess's position. To him it was crucial never to know if she was mad or if everyone else was under the control of a malign influence. Britten felt he had to take sides, and he had decided there was something malign at Bly. Whatever his thoughts about that, Harewood is certain that it was *The Turn of the Screw*, everywhere acclaimed as a great opera, that established Britten's reputation beyond doubt, but Harewood feels that it was one opera too late for him, as it were, to respond to public and critical acclaim; he wanted to do that after *Gloriana* – and he was spurned.

When it came to the *War Requiem*, the notices were ecstatic, but paradoxically that had an adverse effect on Britten because he thought of it as a private work, which people would appreciate and accept, but any idea that it was a popular masterpiece had not crossed his mind. That may have been the cause of his introspection in later years. He then became a person who was wholly gregarious and articulate with his friends, that is with those who were, so to speak, on his side; but with those he did not know or trust he found communication very hard. He became temperamental, sometimes refusing to meet people and being suspicious of them because he was suspicious of success.

At the time when Harewood's first marriage foundered, Britten chose not to see him for three years, feeling it was not politic or appropriate for them to meet. From then on Harewood was no longer part of the inner circle of Britten's musical mentors. He was aware as much as anyone of the shell round the composer protecting him from the outside world – an element hard to reconcile with his essential nature.

Returning to the Covent Garden period, Harewood recalls his connections with two other works of that time: *The Prince of the Pagodas* and *A Midsummer Night's Dream*. Harewood was constantly trying to persuade Britten to write pieces for the house and urging him to conduct there. The ballet was at first intended for the small company at Sadler's Wells, with choreography by John Cranko, but Ninette de Valois encouraged Cranko to arrange it for the larger company at Covent Garden. Harewood coaxed Britten into thinking that was a good idea. In the end, after another conductor had dropped out, Britten conducted the premiere himself. In the case of the opera, Harewood was the one who persuaded the composer to make certain that the work could be given with larger forces at Covent Garden after much smaller scale premiere at the Jubilee Hall at Aldeburgh.

It was at about this period that Harewood tried to get Britten to become musical director at Covent Garden. Harewood felt that, in this way, Britten could make a unique contribution to musical life in Britain, for instance by preparing a Mozart opera and conducting it, going on to another composer's work, and then help revive his own pieces. Britten wavered at one point, but eventually rejected the idea. Harewood now thinks he was probably right in wanting to conserve his powers for composing. Nevertheless, Harewood, who had boundless admiration for him as a conductor, considers that Britten would have conducted Gluck incomparably, and *Falstaff* and *Onegin* too, while in Mozart his brilliance and incisiveness would have been invaluable.

Harewood was also an admirer of Britten's piano playing, but remembers his extreme bouts of nerves before every appearance, even to the extent that he was unable to eat lunch before a concert and would have to spend the time practising. When Harewood inquired if he was still perfecting the fingering, Britten would answer that, if he worked that out in advance, he could not play it at all. He would always phrase the music the same way but never actually play it with the same technique. That was why he was worried if he would be able to play at all when it came to the crunch.

Harewood also recalls his utter professionalism in a series of operatic concerts given in the early days of the English Opera Group when Britten was the accompanist. Joan Cross, Pears, Nancy Evans and Otakar Kraus were among the singers. The programmes were planned and introduced by Harewood. There were extracts from *Così fan tutte*, Verdi, Slav works, English operas, Britten's own works and so on, ending almost invariably with a sequence from *The Beggar's Opera* in Britten's edition. Britten's imaginative playing – the sound he made in such things as the offstage music before the Act 1 duet of *La Traviata*, or in the celebratory music that leads in to the last scene of *Così fan tutte* – was dreamlike. In an all-Verdi concert in the centenary year of 1951 at Aldeburgh, Britten found unerringly the tempi and phrasing apt to music some of which he had probably never thought about before. In rehearsal he had the true creator's insight into how to tackle these pieces. He also knew how to help singers with *their* phrasing – his perception was sometimes quite uncanny, partly because it was all done on the spur of the moment in an almost improvisatory way. Harewood believes that Britten was incapable of doing anything that was unmusical. Any piece of music he touched he adorned. What a pity that he did not play – and record – more. What a pity he was so often inhibited by what he admitted himself were psychosomatic illnesses. On one occasion at Harewood House, a bad shoulder prevented Britten from playing Schubert duets with Josef Krips, although he did partner Krips in an account of the *Liebeslieder Waltzer* – astonishing in view of his poor opinion of Brahms.

On a personal note, Harewood says that those who knew Britten only as the rather reserved and austere artist on the platform would not easily recognize the amusing, jolly person he could be in a friendly circle. He was a witty conversationalist and an exuberant letter-writer, even to the point of being scathing about other people. He was also an adept puncturer of anything pompous in his own surroundings, nor could he bear the notion of being on a pedestal (the reaction to the reception of the *War Requiem* is typical of that). On the other hand, he did not enjoy being debunked or criticized excessively; he did not easily tolerate adverse words written about him or his works. He was a keen games player; he hated to lose at tennis, was annoyed when he had made a poor shot and even more so when his partner made one.

If he trusted someone, he was wonderful company at all sorts of levels. He often stayed at Harewood House, where Princess Mary, Lord Harewood's mother, much liked the composer's company, and he was open and easy with her – a pleasure for them both. Peter Pears and Britten would often give her a small, private recital, just half a dozen Schubert songs that were then in their repertory – not too taxing for anybody.

As an illustration of Britten's ambivalent attitudes to relationships, Harewood recalls on one occasion at Harewood House an encounter with Stephen Spender. It was in the winter of 1952-53. Spender's wife Natasha, who was a close friend of Harewood's first wife Marion, was to give a piano recital at Leeds University. In some ways Britten was reticent about meeting Spender, whom he had known through the Auden connection, but had not seen for some time. Harewood imagined that there must have been some disagreement in the past, that Britten may have wanted to put aside thoughts of his American venture, and that he had committed a solecism in bringing them together again. In the event, Britten was in his most affable mood and the conversation could not have been more lively or friendly. Yet afterwards Britten said that he imagined he had behaved badly, and he had shown that he had been nervous, revealing that he did not really want to see Spender; on Harewood's reckoning, Britten's concern was a complete misreading of what had occurred. Harewood felt that, had Britten not wanted to offend him and his mother, he would have avoided the encounter – but, while Britten was with

Spender, all had been sweetness and light. This incident, small in itself, is perhaps indicative of the privacy Britten felt he needed. Why a man who had great charm and was much sought after should have showed this basic insecurity is hard for Harewood to explain. In the last years of Britten's life this avoidance of contact with people increased greatly, indeed became obsessive.

On one occasion, at a party, a producer showed Britten a notice of one of his works that was fundamentally very favourable, but it had one adjective that offended Britten deeply. Indeed he was so hurt that the party was virtually broken up by the incident, or at least it made Britten retire into his shell. 'This was undoubtedly the obverse side of a man who could demonstrate his deep concern on all occasions for other people's worries – the negative sensibility as opposed to the positive one. It is this personality that may have made Britten the kind of composer he was.'

13

Hans Keller

Hans Keller first heard Britten's music by mistake. After the war he used to attend almost every performance of *Così fan tutte* given by Sadler's Wells Opera. One evening, instead of the overture to Mozart's opera, he found himself listening to something quite strange – it was *Peter Grimes*. He immediately regarded it as a masterpiece. From then on he determined that he would acquaint himself with as much of Britten's music as he could. Indeed, he soon wrote an analysis of the second quartet for *Tempo* – one of his earliest analytical articles in English.

Keller's direct association with the composer began through Britten's reactions to Keller's writings on his music. They had a mutual friend in Erwin Stein, and through him came their first meeting – and a long discussion about sonata structure. The friendship immediately fell into a musical framework, where it remained during subsequent years. That it never transcended that level was Keller's fault, if it can be called a fault. Keller thinks that Britten always felt slightly uncomfortable in an extra-personal relationship.

Britten not only accepted Keller's analysis of the quartets, he also agreed with Keller's reflections, expressed privately, about his approach to sonata structure. Keller then thought that the composer had not altogether solved the problem of development. (Keller is certain that it was because of these conversations that, decades later, Britten dedicated his third quartet to him; all the points then reviewed were treated in the first movement of that work.) The main discussion, as Keller recalls, was about the most important contrast in sonata structure. To begin with it was said to be thematic; after Tovey it became tonal, the contrast between first and second subject key. As important as these points were, Keller averred that the contrast by which sonata structure stood or fell was that between statement and development. He felt this had not been sufficiently realized in the first movement of the second quartet, but feels it *was* achieved, in masterly fashion, in the third.

On other occasions when they talked about music, the discussion was rarely about Britten's own music; it was more usually about Mozart, Beethoven (Britten's ambivalence towards him) and Brahms (less ambivalent!). Keller recalls Britten enunciating his view towards Brahms as follows: 'It's not bad Brahms I mind, it's good Brahms I can't stand.' On Beethoven, he once confessed that, as a boy, he had so closely identified with the composer that he had sometimes had the uncanny feeling that he had written some of the music. Indeed, it was fear of this almost psychotic relationship with Beethoven that produced Britten's hostility – not any failure to appreciate the music.

Keller feels that, with Brahms, Britten resented the lack of spontaneity in the writing, in particular in those passages where Brahms seems to interrupt a melody abruptly in order to avoid what he might have thought of as sentimental writing. Then there are their sound worlds: in this respect they were total opposites. Britten composed with the texture always in his mind, Brahms almost as if he had a grudge against it. Britten seemed in sympathy with his players, whereas Brahms sometimes seemed almost to be composing against them.

Keller found Britten anti-verbal. He found that it took at least an hour until the composer was at all prepared to talk about music. Then, in their discussions, Britten tended to give in. Keller comments, 'That produced a kind of hangover: I did not know how far to trust that "giving-in". He undoubtedly had inhibitions about speaking of his music. When I asked him for articles for *Music Survey*, it took all of two months of pressure to persuade him to contribute. Then when we did receive what he had written (about the *Spring Symphony*) it was vapid. I think he felt in some way guilty about verbalizing.'

Keller translated some of the composer's works into German.

In general, Britten was satisfied with his efforts and in several cases made no alterations. That may be because Keller and he agreed at all points about stresses and shades of verbal sound. Their rapport about the musical side of language was close: if there had to be a choice between beautiful German and musical truth, they were both of the mind that the latter must hold sway.

Keller had the highest regard for Britten as an accompanist (though he was disappointed in his playing of the early Mozart's E flat concerto). He feels that there is no substitute for one creative mind interpreting that of another, and this was the distinctive element in Britten's playing of Schubert. 'It was almost as if he was composing the music there and then – the only comparable experience being Franz Schmidt as pianist and cellist.'

Hans Keller believes that Britten's homosexual nature played an important part in his role as composer, in the sense that the conflicts in his personality contributed powerfully to the tensions in his music. He does not believe, though, that extra-musical emotions can be translated directly into music. Britten was, however, able to capture psychological truths through being homosexual that he would not otherwise have been able to express – for instance in the way he wrote for boys' voices; that is obvious in the sense that nobody had written for them in that manner before. Then he was also able to express the extra-sexual side of heterosexual relationships in a way so-called 'normal' composers could not achieve or have not achieved (for example with Peter Grimes and Ellen Orford) or would have suppressed.

Although, as Keller puts it, 'one cannot write homosexuality into music', he concedes that some things in Britten's music can only be expressed in that way because of his homosexual nature. So far as exclusive relationships between men are concerned, there is a drastic difference between the world of, say, *Siegfried* and of *Billy Budd*, in as much as the latter expresses things that could not have been expressed without an understanding of homosexuality. In sum, Keller believes that Britten's homosexuality had a beneficial influence on his art because it gave him insights into areas of the psyche that he might not have had access to without it. Thus his so-called abnormality was in fact useful to him as a composer: it enabled him to chart territory he would not have otherwise approached.

Keller also has strong views on Britten's preference for writing vocal music. His verbal inspiration was intimately bound up with his ability to create tensions between musical and verbal rhythm; these tensions were of a magnitude that made it possible for him to create extended structures with comparative ease, whereas extended instrumental structures always presented him with certain difficulties. At the same time it is untrue to say that he disliked writing instrumental music; indeed, he regarded it as the supreme challenge, which he faced up to courageously at crucial junctures in his career – last of all in the third quartet.

Keller is quite frank in saying that he was not particularly fond of Britten as a person. He was averse to the conventionality that was often present. Britten could be almost punitively moralistic, as evidenced by his fierce attitude towards the breaking-up of Lord Harewood's first marriage. His pacificism seemed to evade basic human problems. On one occasion, at a dinner party given by Keller and his wife after Britten had returned from Russia, Britten annoyed Keller with his arguments in favour of that country *vis-à-vis* America. This was shortly after the Arab – Israeli war of 1967. Later in the evening, Britten said that the Israelis, rather than going to war, should have lain down in front of the Arab tanks. This was violently objected to not only by Keller but also by Deryck Cooke, a fellow guest. The ensuing dispute led to Britten and Pears making a precipitate departure. It is the only personal row Keller can remember having in his life. 'How odd that it should have been with a pacifist!' The ensuing reharmonization of the relationship was never again disturbed – and what Keller calls 'Britten's aggressive pacifism' was never again touched upon.

Britten's attitude on that occasion seemed to Keller to be typical of a certain glibness and intolerance in the composer particularly in the face of one of the most profound and insoluble problems with which humanity is confronted – the problem of sadism, as distinct from animal aggression.

In his working relationships Britten would be inclined to take up with a person as a performer because he liked them personally, although there might not have been sufficiently strong artistic reasons for doing so; likewise, he might drop them without excuse, musically speaking. That was a pattern that cut across purely artistic requirements.

His home life apart, Britten did not seem to Keller to have the need for very close and involved personal relationships. That may have been part and parcel of a genius's need to spend as much time as he could composing – people had to be kept at a distance. At the same time, Britten was always accessible during the, admittedly occasional, times that they met, and always ready to give of his time where musical matters were concerned. Indeed, it is probably fair to say that, as with Mozart, the central and true personality went into the works.

14

Steuart Bedford

Steuart Bedford got to know Britten through his mother, Lesley Duff, who sang in the first performances of *The Rape of Lucretia* at Glyndebourne in 1946. He and his brothers, David (now a composer) and Peter (singer and producer), spent some time at Glyndebourne that year and the following one, when *Albert Herring* was first produced. Bedford remembers Britten at that time as being approachable and charming (while Peter Pears seemed a bit forbidding, like a schoolmaster) and great fun to be with; he was never thought of as a distinguished or important composer by someone of that age.

At about that time, the Bedford family took a cottage at Snape, and the boys attended many of the early Aldeburgh Festival concerts. Steuart has particular memories of Britten's piano playing then: he was himself learning the piano and was enthralled by the sound Britten drew from the instrument. Britten took sufficient interest in Steuart's musical development to visit him at his preparatory school. He came with Steuart's mother – and sometimes they would bring other distinguished visitors such as E.M. Forster, to whom Steuart remembers playing the piano. In the holidays, Britten played tennis and cricket with the Bedford boys, and was always treated as one of the family. Steuart recalls one famous match at Thorpeness when his father gave Lord Harewood out, much to the latter's chagrin.

Bedford then went to Lancing, where Pears had been at school and for which Britten had written *St Nicholas*. Apart from occasional visits by Britten to school performances, Bedford did not have much contact with the composer for a number of years

Right: Red Square, Moscow, 1963. *Left to right:* Peter Pears, Galina Vishnevskaya, Benjamin Britten, Mstislav Rostropovich and Marion Harewood

Below: Benjamin Britten and Colin Graham at a rehearsal for the English Opera Group production of Britten's realization of *The Beggar's Opera*

Above: Recording Britten's second Parable for Church Performance, *The Burning Fiery Furnace. Left to right:* John Mordler and John Culshaw (Decca), Britten, Robert Tear and John Shirley-Quirk

Left: Britten in the garden of The Red House, Aldeburgh

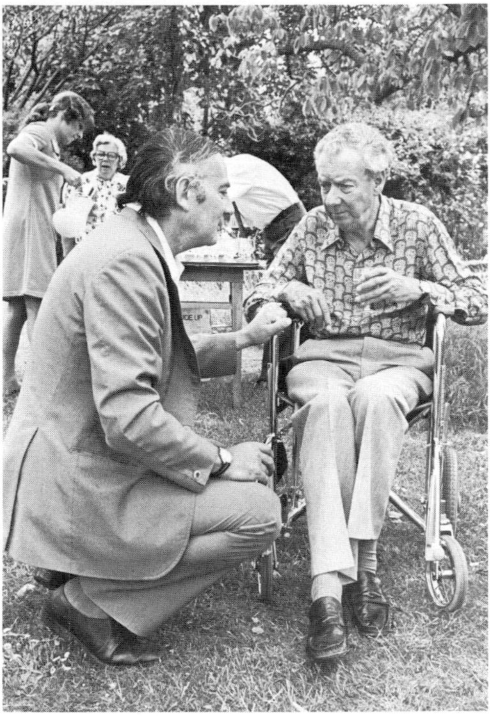

Above left: Benjamin Britten with William Servaes during Britten's last visit to Venice

Above right: Donald Mitchell talking to Britten at a garden party

Right: Britten with Dame Janet Baker and Colin Matthews

Benjamin Britten and Peter Pears in the garden with Murray Perahia

Britten discussing the score of *Phaedra* with Steuart Bedford

thereafter. After he left university, he worked at Glyndebourne on the music staff there, and during that period he went to London to play at a series of auditions for the English Opera Group. Although he did not apply for a job, he was offered one – as a repetiteur – and, very much as an act of faith, he was allowed to conduct *The Beggar's Opera*. Bedford believes that, though Britten was not at the auditions, it was his influence which clinched the job, for at the same time he had been helping the composer with the recording of *A Midsummer Night's Dream*.

From then on, he worked closely with Britten on almost every project. Whether it was he or Britten himself who was conducting, they always made a detailed study of the score in hand. Britten had a very clear idea of what he wanted, how a piece should go, what it should sound like. If Bedford had a question about a musical point, a firm and definite response was always forthcoming. Whenever Britten was preparing an opera of his for stage or recording, he often asked for an effect which, on closer inspection of the score, was confirmed by what he had written. That was a measure of the acuity of his ear, at least until his last illness, when he became a little less certain of himself, and there was a good deal of re-writing after the first performances. He told Bedford that he had never been assailed with so many doubts on earlier occasions.

In preparing a work, the first stage was always a play-through of the complete score, latterly at his Halliford Street house in London, with a few specially selected people present. It could be a tense occasion, with Britten cursing himself for playing so badly. That gave Bedford a clear idea of the general outlines of the work. After that, particularly in the case of *Death in Venice*, which Bedford was always scheduled to conduct, Bedford went closely through each passage with Britten. During the actual rehearsal period of the last opera, Britten was too ill to advise a great deal, although there were plenty of bedside conferences. On earlier occasions, Bedford remembers Britten's extreme practicality in solving problems of technique and balance.

Britten's conducting was, Bedford thinks, remarkable. Because of the respect in which every musician held him, he could draw extraordinary performances from the English

Chamber Orchestra, with which he was particularly happy to work. Because he was so nervous before and during performances, he took a great deal out of himself. Sometimes his ailments were psychosomatic. For a long time he had what was thought to be tennis elbow and his arm was in a sling – the illness developed simply because of his horror at the thought of conducting.

Their last major cooperation was over *Phaedra*, the cantata composed for Janet Baker (q.v.). By the time preparations for that were under way, Britten was sufficiently recovered to be able to listen to rehearsals and to advise Dame Janet and Bedford on interpretation. Although he was physically incapacitated, Britten's mind was as acute as ever in spotting things which needed correction.

In general, Bedford finds that the more he works on Britten's scores, the more carefully he finds they have been marked. There is hardly a vocal line that does not have some meticulous instruction as to how it should be performed, or how it should sound. Even if he was doing a quick rewrite, Britten would automatically add those kind of marks. Such precision can be a terrifying prospect for a singer coming to the music afresh.

Britten was in a technical sense prodigously endowed: there is seldom anywhere where one can fault the balance between voice and orchestra in the operas. Once or twice in *Lucretia* he might have wanted something a little different, but after that one can hardly fault his execution.

Bedford does not recall anything of the first performances of *Albert Herring* at Glyndebourne, but he did hear the premiere of *The Turn of the Screw* on the radio. It was the first score he got to know well.

From the start, Bedford was impressed with the organization of Aldeburgh, and with the breadth of the programmes. Britten and Pears arranged them round their friends, who happened to include a selection of the best musicians, writers, painters and sculptors of the day. That gave the festival its individual flavour, and between them they devised programmes of outstanding merit and interest.

Bedford believes he was favoured as a conductor because he

was always at pains to get to the root of what Britten wanted, and the composer appreciated this scrupulousness. Bedford was also amenable to criticism about whether a piece had been taken too fast or too slow, too soft or too loud, because he had a respect for the composer's notion of how he wanted his own music to sound. Britten was critical of many interpretations he heard of his music. He was intolerant of anything that seemed routine or cavalier, and sometimes would overreact in quite a fierce manner. He was often more tolerant of amateur performances that might not have been technically secure but had the right intent.

He would also react violently against any strong characterization or performance of his music that he did not agree with, considering such an attitude to his work to be arrogant, even if it were not so.

Bedford thought of Britten as a delightful man at heart, but there was much that came between the composer and the outside world. He could not accept the fact that he was a celebrity. He took his responsibilities as a composer very seriously. That made him difficult to approach and those around him protective. Maybe that masked the true man for beneath the mask there was undoubtedly a gentle, human personality.

15

Miss Hudson

Miss Hudson was housekeeper at Crag House and then the Red House from 1948 until 1973. She got to know Britten well before the Second World War when he bought her uncle's mill at Snape; after this, being interested in the piano, she watched out for concerts in public or on the radio in which he was to take part. One day when she was in the Aldeburgh dairy shop, she heard that a new housekeeper was wanted by Benjamin Britten at Crag House. At that point she has no idea that he was living in the vicinity. Her predecessor thought she would be just the person to take over. So an appointment was made for her to see Britten and Pears, and she took the job.

She immediately found them, and the post, congenial. Britten was very easy-going. If she was ordering anything, he would say to her, 'Do what you like, Miss Hudson.' She would then suggest something and ask, 'Is that what you would really like?' He would answer 'I'd prefer so-and-so.' And she would say, 'Well then, have it.' Having looked after an elderly father and a brother for whom she had acted as a mother, she felt she was doing the same in her new job. 'I always gave in to them, and never "went opposite" them, so relations were always easy.'

She recalls Britten often getting up at six o'clock, going for a walk with Clytie, their dog and her son Joey, both dachshunds. Or he would set to work. Britten liked simple food but he liked his meals 'nice', as she puts it – in other words lovingly prepared by her. If Pears had been away and was expected home, Britten and she would often alter dinner so as to choose something that he would particularly like. There was a great deal of entertaining, often with musical guests who might be working on a

Britten composition. 'He was always writing an opera,' she says. As the years went by, the staff increased and Miss Hudson was required to keep the peace. There were also more and more guests. On occasion Britten would ask her quizzically whether he should take them to the Festival Club or bring them home. She knew very well that he wanted them to come to the Red House, and was prepared to meet his wishes.

Before a concert he was always nervous and she used to prepare him Complan. After it, he would eat a good dinner. Britten was fond of roast beef, creamy rice puddings and spotted dog. 'Nursery food,' Miss Hudson describes it.

In the morning he always had a cold bath and in the evening a hot one, and during the day there was plenty of swimming when the weather allowed. In later years Miss Hudson would warn him against swimming too much, but he felt that it did him nothing but good. In earlier years at the Red House he played a great deal of tennis, often at weekend parties.

She considers that he never gave himself enough rest. After exercise in the afternoon, he would usually work through until 8.00 when dinner was served, and often go to his study again after that. Pencil and paper were seldom out of his hands. When he was working, he hated to be interrupted.

She had a cheque book and was trusted to take charge of everything; occasionally Britten and Pears would have spurts of looking into things, but most of the time Miss Hudson was left on her own to manage their affairs as she wished. She believes that she was an economical housekeeper. 'I was meaner with their money than I was with my own.' Similarly the gardener was more or less left to his own devices – until one day Pears and Britten would come out and suddenly want a re-ordering of things.

At Christmas, Britten always did the carving. Miss Hudson recalls his telling her that, as a boy, he always had to carve the turkey simply because he was so good at that – as at everything else. One of her helpers once came out of the dining room saying, 'I wish my husband could carve a joint like Mr Britten. He would make it go twice as far.' Britten liked a traditional Christmas: there was always a large ham, plum pudding, cakes with icing, mince pies.

He hardly ever read the newspapers. Usually he saw *The Times* but, if something appeared in it that he disapproved of, he switched to the *Guardian*. There were few magazines, but *House and Garden* was usually bought for her.

He was 'very particular' about his clothes and she was responsible for making sure everything was clean and as it should be. Shirts were specially made for both Britten and Pears by Austin Reed, and they had to be washed at home.

He loved his cars and she still remembers an old Rolls that he had when she first knew him. Then there was the famous Alvis in which he loved to go round the countryside with the sliding roof open. He also loved his dogs and, at the end, Gilda – who is now Miss Hudson's – often lay beside him on his bed.

16

Norman Del Mar

Norman Del Mar came to work with Britten through Erwin Stein, who had heard him conducting various works on the nascent Third Programme. On Stein's recommendation, Del Mar was invited to Aldeburgh to meet the composer, who was looking for a conductor for *Let's Make an Opera* and a general assistant for the young festival. 'He showed me the score of *Let's Make*, and sounded me out about my views on how this new kind of piece should be presented. I suppose Britten was trying to assess how I would be able to handle the work, to stand up in front of the audience and make a success of encouraging them to participate.'

The meeting was an undoubted success: Del Mar was invited to the 1949 festival not only to be in charge of *Let's Make* and *The Rape of Lucretia* but for about as much work as he could manage, including playing with Manoug Parikian at a recital.

Britten was, of course, present when *Let's Make* was first read through at Erwin Stein's house in London, and with the librettist Eric Crozier he gave his views of the piece. During the actual preparation of the production he hardly interfered at all, but was available to be a father-confessor should anyone want to refer to him. Indeed, he would often improvise or rewrite parts there and then. Later, Del Mar discovered that Britten could be unhappy about some aspect on interpretation, but was ever loath to make criticisms on the spot. 'On occasion, he would take me for a long walk, and it would then emerge that, for example, I had not been quite strict enough in this or that respect. You could go wrong without knowing it.'

From the very first *Let's Make* worked well. Del Mar's spontaneity and elan in 'rehearsal' broke the ice at once. After the first half of the premiere, Britten insisted that Del Mar have a bath while he changed for the second. He stayed with the conductor and spoke to him in eulogistic fashion about his contribution. Britten said there was no limit to what they might achieve had he (Del Mar) a mind to do it. That was a humble and touching moment.

Those early days at Aldeburgh, Del Mar recalls, were full of enthusiasm. Indeed there was a slight danger that the festival might just become one big private party. There was no doubt that they were all at the feet of someone who had something very special about him.

Del Mar never had a formal appointment to the festival nor to the English Opera Group, but there is no doubt that he was the major musical figure in the Britten entourage during those years. He worked on all the operas, both Britten's and anyone else's. He prepared *The Beggar's Opera* in Britten's version, Brian Easdale's *The Sleeping Children*, Arthur Oldham's *Love in a Village*. Although he was never in on the planning of festivals, when the itinerary had been prepared, he was the general who carried out the orders implicitly.

Early on there was one near-break in Del Mar's relationship with Britten, when he was asked to conduct *Let's Make* in New York. 'I accepted with the composer's blessing. The work was to be produced on Broadway, where opera had never been a success. Out of New York it went well, but in town it was torn to shreds by the theatre critics, and I was heckled. It hardly lasted a week. When news of this ill-starred venture reached Britten's ear, he was shocked because he was told that I had abandoned the EOG to further my own ambitions in America. It seemed a betrayal when it was nothing of the sort. My explanations were eventually accepted, and I continued my work as before.'

In fact Del Mar's eventual break with Britten also arose from a disagreement over *Let's Make*. As the years went by, the work became rather divorced from the main part of the EOG programme; it was being treated as a seasonal work, as a kind of Christmas pantomime. Del Mar thought that was wrong in principle, partly because it frequently involved him in directing it in big theatres where he was in danger of becoming as much compere as conductor. Del Mar insisted that he must remain in the pit. Britten took offence at this attitude, suggesting that Del Mar perhaps wanted only to do the 'juicy things' and not the hard work. That might mean that their association would have to lapse. Again it seemed as if Del Mar had offended him without intending to; indeed he had been trying to defend Britten's artistic aims, by keeping up standards. Del Mar realized his days were numbered: that was the pattern of things, but the way it happened did hurt Del Mar at the time. Later there was, as with others, a reconciliation, and he was asked to record *Noyes Fludde*; it was as if there had been no break.

Del Mar had great admiration for Britten as a conductor, and still treats the composer's interpretations on record of his own work with great reverence. Britten remained remarkably faithful to his own instructions, and those instructions themselves give a very clear idea of how he wanted his music to sound. Britten's documentation of his intentions is invaluable to Del Mar, who always tried to model his own readings on them. Everything Britten did was extremely skilful, because as a performer and as a composer he was thoroughly professional. As a player, everything was instinctively musical – something one learnt to appreciate greatly.

Del Mar was grateful, and honoured, to be asked back at one of the last festivals during Britten's lifetime to conduct his Suite drawn from *The Prince of the Pagodas*. Britten was obviously still sad that the original concept of the work had not quite succeeded, that something had left a sour taste in the mouth over the cooperation with Cranko. Anthony Gishford of Boosey's had asked Del Mar to prepare a suite. Del Mar's first ideas were not acceptable to Britten, who diffidently suggested some of his own, which Del Mar eagerly accepted. The Suite had its first performance with Del Mar conducting at the 1961 Edinburgh Festival. This was never published during Britten's lifetime in case Britten himself wanted to make his own arrangement from the ballet. The composer also felt that something from Act 2 should be included (Del Mar had excluded that act from his Suite). He also felt that Del Mar's ending was a bit abrupt – a problem that has not yet been solved.

Nobody is better placed than Del Mar, who is familiar with almost all Britten's compositions from the inside, as it were, to make a judgement on the opus. At first he was worried by certain aspects: the occasional thinness of the scoring and the almost mechanical use of certain devices – for example, in *The Rape of Lucretia*, the way Brittten presents a theme, then turns it upside down. This constant inversion ends up by seeming like a trick. In *Peter Grimes* there are points where he seems to be marking time: during recitative passages a single chord is endlessly repeated, while those on stage indulge in rapid parlando. Now he accepts these kind of devices as part of a total picture that at the time he could not see.

Del Mar remembers the curious fact that, when each work came out, Britten's colleagues would comment that here was an inevitable step downhill; yet, when the one after that appeared, they came to realize that the piece previously denigrated had become part of the total *oeuvre* and had been accepted. In other words, the first impact would be disappointing, but later the work in question would fall into place as a substantial addition to Britten's output.

More serious failings, in Del Mar's opinion, are the slightly detached attitude felt in big love scenes and the occasional sense that the composer is trying to be clever – a charge which Britten bitterly resented. He wanted to be considered a natural and profound musician, but so often the remark that most easily and spontaneously came to mind was, 'How brilliant!' When pressed, Del Mar says that the most wholly successful works were some of the early ones such as *Les Illuminations*, the second string quartet, and the *Serenade for Tenor, Horn and Strings*; they stand up as masterpieces at any level. So does a great deal of *Grimes*. Another work that Del Mar totally accepts is the arrangement of *The Beggar's Opera*, which has unaccountably fallen from the repertory.

Britten's choice of other people's music during the festivals with which Del Mar was concerned was often unexpectedly eclectic. For example, Del Mar conducted Wagner's *Siegfried Idyll*, Schoenberg's chamber symphony, Chausson's 'concerto' for violin, piano and string quartet, the Grieg piano concerto, Gerhard's piano concerto. The choice was wide-ranging and often unexpected. It was perhaps indicative of Britten's broad knowledge of an appreciable repertory. As the festival expanded, it became rather less personal, and less of a 'private party'. That was bound to happen and there was no harm in it; indeed it was a healthy development. But the early years had a special enthusiasm and spontaneity about them, almost a sense of improvisation, that Del Mar recalls with pleasure. His association with Britten in a still-formative time in his career is remembered gratefully. That it had to come to an end was perhaps inevitable, but no less regrettable all the same.

17

Mary Potter

Mary Potter, with her husband Stephen, owned the Red House at Aldeburgh before Britten and Pears occupied it. She came to know Pears through her paintings – he had more interest in art than Britten, whom at first she tended to avoid as being too intellectual for her. Her husband was an eager golfer. On one occasion they invited many of his golfing companions to a cocktail party. Britten and Pears were also among the guests and Britten seemed rather lost among the uncongenial company. When Mrs Potter caught his eye, he suddenly asked, 'How's the work?' Immediately she realized that he was the one person in the room, other than Peter, with whom she had something in common.

Almost at once they achieved rapport. With Pears being away a great deal of the time on professional engagements, and her husband working in London midweek, Mrs Potter became one of the composer's nearest friends. They agreed that, when the other's housekeeper had the night off, they would dine with each other. They often went on long walks together, played tennis and swam, and it was Britten who persuaded the Potters to turn the bowling green at the Red House into a tennis court.

Eventually, after Mrs Potter and her husband parted, she and the composer agreed to exchange houses. Britten and Pears wanted the Red House passionately for their home at that time; Crag House on the Aldeburgh seafront was too exposed to casual visitors. The idea was that after a year they should build Mrs Potter a studio on a piece of land they had bought beside the Red House; she moved there in 1963.

At first Britten did not take a great deal of interest in her paintings. His eye for art at that time was mostly on the old masters. But, as the years went by, he became more and more receptive to modern works and to hers in particular, so that she came to value his opinion of her paintings almost more than anyone else's. As with other subjects, once he became involved, he was concerned to make himself an expert in it.

He also wanted her to share his enthusiasms. When she was already in her fifties, he persuaded her to accompany him and Pears on a skiing holiday, and insisted that she should learn to ski. After breaking a tooth when she fell over on her first trial, she gave it up, and returned to painting. Where music was concerned, she could not pretend fully to comprehend all his work, but she did play the recorder and Britten duly wrote her a piece for three recorders on that holiday, calling it *Alpine Suite*. Britten insisted that she practise the instrument if she was not going to ski. Indeed, every day she would practise with Britten and Pears on the sections that he had written the evening before, to the extent that others in the chalet began to complain of the noise.

Although she believes that he offered friendship, even affection, to many people, there were occasions when for some reason he would take against a person at a first meeting. That person may have been in awe of meeting a well-known man and made some foolish remark. Later, Britten would come to realize, often through Mrs Potter's persuasion, that he had made a mistake. He would then regret his first reaction and try to make amends. In contrast, he would not realize until afterwards that some person had taken advantage of him.

In spite of their close friendship, she would never presume to take any kind of advantage of it. They both respected the other's working curriculum. Neither would telephone the other between nine o'clock and lunchtime – a period considered sacrosanct for work. If there was a need to contact her in this time, Britten would always make deep apologies for the disturbance. There might be a drink before lunch, then a walk after it. Between tea and dinner there would be another period of intense work for the composer. In the evening Britten would often read, and he and Mrs Potter would exchange books that they had enjoyed.

On walks and other occasions, Britten showed absorbing interest in bird life, but very little in flowers. Often there were long periods of silence, often long discussions about working methods and the reasons why one worked. She can recall his once coming round to her studio when she was regretting that she had just taken out the best thing in a painting – at which he commented that he was always doing that in a composition. In addition to these practical discussions and exchanges of view, there were talks on the relationship between working hard, creating things, life style and getting on with other people.

She found Britten had charming manners. He would always be polite while someone was present, even if, rather naughtily, he might curse them when they had gone. Although she was a constant smoker, she would never indulge herself at the Red House where smoking was more or less forbidden. Even on the many holidays together with Britten and Pears, she would be careful not to smoke in their presence.

Unless they were abroad, Britten and Pears always invited Mary Potter for Christmas Day and she would reciprocate the hospitality on Boxing Day. Britten liked to make the same jokes each year. When the pudding came in, with the brandy alight, he would comment that it was not the Napoleon, only the Remy Martin. It was almost a 'family tradition'. In early days, E.M. Forster was a pretty regular visitor at Christmas too; and Imogen Holst was sometimes among the company.

Relationships with his own family fluctuated. Beth was probably closest to him, his brother Robert most distant. He took a keen interest in his nephews and nieces, always concerned about what they were doing.

He treated Mrs Potter as somebody on whom he could rely for consolation when he was miserable. He could turn to her when he received adverse criticism and expect sympathy; he could turn to her after *Death in Venice* had been completed under the most stressful conditions, when he realized that he was more ill than he had thought and must be operated on at once.

She travelled extensively with Britten and Pears. Although when abroad he was concerned about what he ate, Britten was an easy companion on these holidays. Mrs Potter recalls them all with pleasure, but she remembers in particular one extensive journey through Germany, Switzerland, then on to Venice and back through France. On one part of the return journey they were waiting for a train high up in the Alps between Italy and France, which had been delayed by ice. At the station Britten had to retire to the lavatory. Suddenly the train arrived and Peter called out to Britten to come out. Britten replied that he could hear it but as there was no paper he had first to decide which letter to use. The train had to wait for the decision.

After his operation, Britten often confessed to Mrs Potter, though probably to few others, that he was profoundly depressed and that he found life hardly worth living. He fretted about his disability, hated to be dependent on others and bitterly regretted not being able to work at full stretch. Up to the time of his illness, he was pretty tough and very active, although when he played tennis he was always aware that a valve in his heart was troubling him. When he said he did not want to take part in the final set, he meant it; he was not just saying so out of politeness to his guests, but because he felt something was not quite right. Possibly for the same reason he was a cautious bather, but it was more likely that this was because he was wary of uncertain currents and the like, particularly when holidaying in Brittany and swimming in supposedly prohibited places.

She remains eternally grateful for his friendship, and misses his daily coming and goings. 'Today, when I hear his music and its depth of emotions, I often wonder how they could come from a man who was in so many ways cheerful and light-hearted. It was perhaps because he was, deep down, acutely aware of the misery and sadness in the world. Cruelty upset him so much that he had to cry out against it in his music.'

On the cover of her copy of *Alpine Suite* is inscribed the following:

To darling Mary: a tiny memento of a perilous journey, the results of which have made the world so much richer – and I mean visually.

Lots of love. Ben. 1956.

18

Rosamund Strode

Having studied singing and the viola at the Royal College of Music immediately after the war (gaining Exhibitions for singing), Rosamund Strode realized that she would probably not make the grade as an executant and went for two years to Dartington under Imogen Holst (q.v.), where she thought of training to become a county music adviser. But, as a result of singing in concerts given at Dartington, she changed her mind, and decided to try to become a professional singer after all, taking private lessons in London from Julian Kimbell. She was a founder member of the Purcell Singers, the small choir that Imogen Holst (by then working in Aldeburgh) had formed at Britten's request at the end of 1952, as a group to take part in the Aldeburgh Festival and perform on other occasions. From time to time Rosamund Strode was asked by Miss Holst (who of course knew her capabilities) to help with the festival and other work, especially in connection with choral and orchestral music.

The festival then had virtually no staff, apart from the general administrator Stephen Reiss (q.v.) and a part-time secretary, and there was nobody except Imogen Holst herself to see to the preparation of the music; help was therefore very necessary. Rosamund Strode had already met Britten at Dartington in 1948, when Peter Pears and he had given a recital there (even earlier, as a young student, she had collected their autographs!) and Britten conducted an early performance of *St Nicholas* at Dartington at that time. There, too, Rosamund Strode had once played the viola alongside the composer, when he joined a weekly orchestral practice conducted by Imogen Holst.

The first serious work Miss Strode did on Britten's own music was in 1956, when Imogen Holst asked her to come to Aldeburgh and rule bar lines for one act of the full score of *The Prince of the Pagodas* – a huge score. (It took three days to do just one act!) From then on she became increasingly involved at Aldeburgh, while at the same time continuing her musical career in London, and organizing a boys' choir (which became the London Boy Singers), again at Britten's request.

In 1963, Rosamund Strode went to work at Aldeburgh on a more permanent basis. Britten suggested that she might like to work for him with Imogen Holst (with the long-term view of eventually succeeding her as his musical assistant) and at the same time help with the musical side of the festival. At first she used to go to Aldeburgh for three days a week, returning to London thereafter, but it soon turned into four – and eventually became a full-time job. In 1964, the thirtieth anniversary of Gustav Holst's death, his daughter became increasingly involved with the work concerning her father's music, and accordingly Rosamund Strode became 'official' music assistant to Britten in that year, a little sooner than anticipated.

By this time there was a considerable backlog of Britten's scores awaiting publication, and there were always new pieces to be prepared. These jobs had to be done in the latter part of the year, up to Christmas. The first half of each year was usually concerned with the preparation and editing of music for the festival, including those works by other composers that Britten was to conduct – for instance, putting his marks into the instrumental parts (and often spending hours cleaning up the copies first!), a matter over which he was very particular.

In the case of his own compositions, Britten cared very much about the actual look of the music on the page; everything had to be clear and easy to read and use. He had definite views about how it was to be printed, reading proofs with great care. He also kept copies with up-to-date corrections marked on them, so that at subsequent reprintings the text could be put right.

Composing did not come easily to Britten, and the reason new works were not always published at once was his need to be free to make any changes he felt necessary. He wanted a work to 'settle down' before it went to the publisher, and was only too aware of the trouble and expense involved in making alterations to a piece already published.

Britten kept a strict composing routine, and his staff were careful not to interrupt him and to respect his privacy as a creative artist. A great deal of concentrated thought preceded the actual writing of a piece; having got a passage down on paper Britten would play it over on the piano, reworking it if necessary until he was satisfied – sometimes quite a lengthy process.

Rosamund Strode often acted as a page-turner for Britten when he was playing the piano at concerts. Perhaps it was an advantage that she was not herself a pianist – not, as it were, watching his every move. He was a real musician's pianist, not just a player of the instrument; his left hand, in particular, had something very special about it. She recalls Viola Tunnard saying that it was no good trying to match Britten's piano tone in duets: he had a way of making the hammers move differently from other pianists – and 'how *dare* he!'

It has to be remembered that Britten was, from an early age, a highly proficient pianist, passing the Associated Board Grade VIII examination with distinction when he was only twelve. As a young man he became thoroughly familiar with a wide range of piano works and tackled the very difficult bravura solo part at the premiere of his own piano concerto at a Promenade concert (conducted by Sir Henry Wood) in 1938. In later life he continued to give public performances as an incomparable accompanist and player of chamber music – a career that continued until his disablement after the heart operation in 1973, when his right hand became affected by the slight stroke he then suffered.

Rosamund Strode found that one always knew where one was with Britten. He was decisive but never dictatorial; everything was managed in a courteous, civilized way – and, although he could (rarely) lose his temper, the storm passed very quickly. Benjamin Britten was an inspiration to, and made demands upon, all those who worked with him, pushing them up to and beyond what they considered to be their own limits. But, as he made no fewer demands on himself, the effort to attain his high standards was uniquely worthwhile and satisfying.

19

Basil Coleman

Basil Coleman's association with Britten began when he was asked by Tyrone Guthrie to help the singers with the dialogue of *The Beggar's Opera*. At that time Coleman was an out-of-work actor looking for some different outlet in the theatrical field. Then Guthrie invited Coleman to be his assistant and begin to work on certain scenes. From the start Coleman found he was entirely in rapport with Britten, an engrossing and enchanting person who went out of his way to be pleasant and friendly. This was flattering to Coleman, who at that stage did not, of course, know him well.

Although Coleman had already been fascinated by some of Britten's song cycles, he had not heard any of the operas when he began to work on *The Beggar's Opera*. Britten must have observed Coleman's contributions there, for he was very soon asked to produce *The Little Sweep*. That led on to the production of Britten's other operas, described by Basil Coleman in *The Operas of Benjamin Britten*.[1] Having gained the composer's confidence, Coleman was given his head, and Britten seldom interfered with his style of staging the works, or had much of a disagreement with him about them.

After *The Turn of the Screw* in 1954, Coleman left the Britten fold and spent the best part of ten years in Canada; during that time he kept in close touch with Britten and Pears, and when he returned he became involved in the televised productions of Britten's operas, beginning with the hugely successful *Billy*

[1] Hamish Hamilton, 1979

Budd, staged in the studio. After that, he was anxious to do *Peter Grimes* in the same way, but Britten was insistent that it be televised at the Maltings, Snape, and did not accept Coleman's argument that, outside Television Centre, he might be confronted by restricted space, cameras in fixed positions and a technical staff unfamiliar with the needs of opera. Coleman was overruled. Britten's thinking was quite understandable. Besides being nearer home, he would be able to conduct the opera in the same place as it was being performed (whereas in the studio, the orchestra has to be elsewhere, causing difficulties in liaison), and the sound quality would be improved by exploiting the remarkable acoustics of the Maltings. Similarly, Pears felt that, unless he was in direct touch with the orchestra, he could not phrase in the way he wished. In the end Coleman withdrew from directing *Grimes*; he considers that it became a stage production televised rather that a production conceived in television terms (as *Budd* undoubtedly was), and was not alone in thinking that the sound was little improvement on that achieved in the studio because of the poor quality of the receiving sets. Coleman's withdrawal upset Britten.

Years earlier, Britten had promised Coleman that he would compose a television opera for him. That was the seed from which *Owen Wingrave* grew: Coleman had told the BBC authorities about Britten's idea and, following the success of *Budd*, Britten was persuaded to write *Wingrave*. Coleman, having in the meantime become somewhat estranged from Britten over *Grimes*, was not invited to produce it when the time came. Later, however, composer and producer were reconciled and Britten is known to have said, 'That was a stupid business; Basil and I were both right!' Coleman himself considers that Britten was right in the sense that he was always happier working 'in his own kingdom', but from the point of view of technical and visual success he holds his ground. Britten undoubtedly felt that he wanted to prove there was nothing that the Maltings could not do, and John Culshaw, who had by then become head of music on BBC-TV, wanted to prove himself in his new position.

Coleman has cherished personal recollections of Britten. He

remembers that on one occasion, when he himself was close to having a nervous breakdown, Britten insisted on his coming to Aldeburgh and made him talk over all his difficulties. After that, he left Coleman alone, while keeping a close watch on him for a couple of days to ensure that he was all right. That was the extent of his kindness and concern.

At work he was tough on himself and on others. He could also be ruthless, but one was always enriched by his presence. His sense of theatre was uncanny, and he immediately realized if something was not progressing in the right way. If an effect was not as strong as he wished, he would always suggest an alternative.

Britten was a superb talker, as Coleman remembers him. He recalls many evenings of overheard discussions between the composer and E. M. Forster before *Billy Budd*. Then there was Britten's love of nature and of church buildings. On one occasion he made a sudden decision to go on a picnic to a certain spot because a nightingale was said to have been heard there. Britten was incredibly responsive to all country sounds and to such phenomenon as the play of light on the landscape: he never missed the slightest change. On such occasions Coleman had to know when not to talk, when Britten needed to commune with himself or with nature to allow musical ideas to develop.

Britten once told Coleman that he really required three lives: one to play the piano, another to compose, another in which to become a champion tennis-player. Like other friends, Coleman confirms that Britten was a tense and competitive sportsman and as such hated to lose. His playing had the same kind of incisiveness and precision as much of his music. He seldom wasted his time playing with Coleman, who was considered a 'bad fourth'. Pears, Mary Potter and Laurens van der Post were more regular partners.

Latterly, the two were once again intimate friends. Coleman spent Britten's last Christmas with the composer, a memory that he will always treasure. Britten's nurse, Rita Thomson, told Coleman that the composer had already confided in her that Coleman would have been a guest at Christmas 1976, a visit that, alas, was never to be.

Britten's principles were, Coleman thinks, an important part of his make-up. Although he grew more conservative as the years passed, he never lost his concern for people and causes. He was also strong on morals, increasingly so as he became older. His pacificism was part of the same syndrome.

Coleman emphasizes the Englishness of Britten's music. He produced *A Midsummer Night's Dream* in Buenos Aires and San Francisco, and in both places he was struck in the last scene by the congruence of the music with English church bells. So moved was he at this point on both occasions that he felt profoundly homesick. Naturally, he feels most empathy with all those operas that he has staged: *The Rape of Lucretia*, which he produced at Aldeburgh, and, in 1976, *Albert Herring*, for Danish Television, in Danish, as well as the operas which he produced in the first place. Then there was *Peter Grimes* in the second Sadler's Wells production, dating from the early sixties. Britten never saw this – simply, Coleman believes, because his enormous loyalty to Pears always made him reticent about seeing somebody else in Pears's parts; in this case Ronald Dowd played Grimes.

Britten had a tremendous sense of humour, was amusing company, and often made fun of himself. He had a marvellous devotion to his dachshunds, who always accompanyed him on his long walks, when he would help them over difficult places. This is another demontration of his uncanny sensitivity to the needs of anything around him. He was equally responsive to ideas, and this quick wit – part of his living life to the full – made him tire easily. He was also easily concerned about his own health; even if some illnesses were psychsomatic, he obviously felt genuinely unwell – there was no question of it being mere hypochondria.

He was loath to meet anybody with whom he might not be on good terms. Once, Coleman wanted to please a theatrical colleague by introducing him to the composer; Britten agreed but, when it came to it, Britten reneged on his promise. For him, there would be no point in the occasion, because it would not lead to anything.

He had a true sense of when and where to appear, and he also had a gift for theatrical timing. He knew when to accept awards and honours: Coleman is convinced he accepted a peerage – an event that worried many friends – because he knew it was an honour done to British music as much as to him as a person. Similarly, when commissioning works to be performed by the English Opera Group, of which Coleman was at one time artistic director, Britten was very conscious of the direction in which he wanted the company to progress.

He tended to remain in Aldeburgh because he felt restless away from his own surroundings and was worn out by things to which he was not accustomed. Socializing was, by the same token, anathema to him. When he returned to Aldeburgh after a journey to London, it took him at least a day to return to his normal way of life. Part of that life was his settled routine, much aided by Miss Hudson (q.v.), with whom he had a wonderful relationship: she adored him and they were able to talk about a great number of things. At the end there was Rita, who kept him going during the last years and with whom he shared many in-jokes.

The fisherman Bill Burrell was another intimate of the composer. He went on a trip up the Rhine with Coleman, composer Arthur Oldham and Pears during 1951. Bill and his brother were in charge of the boat, a converted naval motor-launch. They went across the North Sea, then up the river – an enterprising venture. Britten was the life and soul of the party, observant of every detail. Food was bought on the way. The cooking was done mostly by Pears and Coleman; Britten, not a discriminating eater, was no cook. It was a revelatory trip to make just before *Billy Budd*. At this time, when Britten and Pears still lived on the front at Aldeburgh, Burrell visited the house whenever he liked, blowing in like a breath of fresh air; he was admired by Britten because he did not pretend to be anything but what he was. Nobody gave Britten so much joy when he arrived on the scene – a true friend.

Burrell's children were later always welcome at the Red House, as were the offspring of all Britten's friends because the composer always had an exceptional rapport with young people. He fed off them, as it were, but Coleman is sure that *they* were always exhilarated by the experience of meeting *him*.

'In his professional life he had a similar kind of rapport with singers. If he saw that they were committed wholeheartedly to him, there was nothing he would not do to encourage them, and they felt they could give of their best with the composer there to support them. The performances when Britten was conducting were always special occasions for everyone concerned, and nobody knew better than he whether or not an evening had been successful. And how unhappy, even angry, he was when something went wrong that should not have gone wrong! By the same token, he himself knew better than anyone where the weaknesses lay in his own works, and would also commend to me those that he considered good. Listening to his works with him was also interesting: he was at all times eager to know what the audience's response would be. If someone made a constructive comment, he showed gratitude – as he did if an artist's cooperation in a performance had been to his liking. He was always generous about another man's creative work, none more so than mine; I consider myself privileged to have known and worked with Britten.'

20

Colin Graham

Colin Graham got to know Britten through the English Opera Group. Once he had decided to abandon an acting career, Graham wrote to every opera and ballet company in the country asking for a job as a stage manager, so that he could watch other directors at work and gain technical knowledge. After several abortive efforts, he finally found work with the English Opera Group, which needed an assistant stage manager for performances in the West Country of Britten's adaptation of *The Beggar's Opera*; this enabled Graham to show his talents as a stage manager to the full as the piece involves so many scene changes and rearrangements of props. That was in 1953 and, for the rest of the year, Graham – though not yet engaged by the company – helped stage various *ad hoc* programmes for it. During that year, he saw Britten but did not actually meet him. The following year he worked on *The Rape of Lucretia* for the Schwetzingen Festival, then went off to Venice to stage-manage the premiere of *The Turn of the Screw*. In the meantime, and in preparation for that event, Graham had taught himself Italian. With virtually nobody else speaking Italian, he was called in to mediate with the recalcitrant stage staff at the Fenice. He did that so effectively that the following year he became the EOG's stage director. By then the original company producer, Basil Coleman (q.v.), had emigrated to Canada, and Graham took over staging the many revivals of the opera.

Britten was the conductor at the premiere of *The Turn of the Screw*, and Graham was interested to see that he worked with Basil Coleman very much on equal terms; that is, he did not in any way lay down the law about his own work. Every scene had obviously been discussed in depth before rehearsals began, and Graham subsequently found that this was always the case. There was a very close rapport between Britten, his producer and his singers – and, as Graham was later to discover, at an earlier stage with the librettist.

Graham came closer to Britten on the way to Stratford, Ontario, for the festival there in 1956. On the ship, Britten and Pears were travelling first-class, the rest were travelling tourist. One day Graham was invited to the first-class deck to have discussions about *Noyes Fludde*. Britten asked him whether he thought he could produce it. The composer had been impressed with how Graham had dealt with each new boy in the role of Miles and said this new piece was to have nine principal children and a chorus of two hundred. Would he be able to manage them all? Britten wanted there to be a degree of naivety about the whole thing; for that reason he may have been prepared to take a chance. He had had his spies out, among them Joan Cross, watching Graham's productions for the Park Lane Group, so he was aware of Graham's promise.

It was while preparing *Noyes Fludde* in 1957-8 that Graham discovered the first stage was a full discussion of the libretto with Britten – in this case the edited version of the Chester Miracle Plays. Britten was eagerly concerned with every detail of how the work would transfer into opera, and at one point Graham was required to write a verse for one of the songs. This illustrates Britten's practicality as a stage person. And, from the very start of their working relationship, Graham was aware of the composer's ever-open mind to ideas. He never had a preconceived notion about how an opera would look. He would explain his musical concept and the character of a work, but he would not project a visual idea, although he had a strongly developed visual sense. On the other hand, it was important for the composer to know before composition what the original concept was likely to be. Hence the intensive early discussions.

Graham designed the set for *Noyes Fludde*, and took it to Britten with some trepidation. Expecting to have it shot down in flames, Graham was delighted to find that, in fact, it was received enthusiastically and provoked much constructive thinking from Britten. As soon as he saw something visually stimulating in front of him, Britten started thinking about it in terms of the opera. It was the same with the church operas, although the problems there were different. The set had to allow an instrumentalist or singer to lead all the time but, once the set had been devised to allow for that, Britten kept it before him while he was writing. *Curlew River* was written in Venice. Every evening he would discuss in depth with Graham the section he was to write the following day, down to such details as where people were going to stand and relationships between the characters, so that he could say that if that person was standing in a particular place he could give the cue to another.

A Midsummer Night's Dream was produced not by Graham but by the choreographer John Cranko, whose methods seemingly did not go down too well with the composer. Choreographers like to improvise stage movement to the music in rehearsal, and that gave the composer the impression, perhaps mistaken, that Cranko had not done his homework. Britten would not forgive anyone who did not know their notes or failed to obey dynamic marks – and so on. He was so meticulous himself that he expected others to be the same, though paradoxically he liked people to be flexible. In Graham's early days of production he would work out the action in great detail beforehand, but Britten urged him always to be there and to change things if it was necessary – that is what Britten would do with his music: if, in consultation with others, he felt that a passage was too short or too long, he would go away and rewrite it.

It was natural, however, that Britten was often not happy with later productions of his work with which he had not been intimately concerned. He confessed to Graham towards the end of his life that he had the sight and sound of the first production embedded in him and anything that clashed with that was an aggravation. He conceded that it may have been a weakness on his part – and he liked to think of himself as broad-minded – but, once something had, after much effort, been fixed in his mind, he found it hard to see how there could be improvements on it, unless there had been elements about the premiere with which he disagreed. The fact that he had been unhappy with the first *Dream*, and with the Covent Garden staging and casting that followed, meant that when Graham came to produce it he was able to cooperate with Britten on 'getting it right'. Although Britten was not present when Graham did a new production of *The Rape of Lucretia* for the Edinburgh Festival, he was happy in that case with Graham's concept. He was not so pleased with the new *Albert Herring*, a work that in any case had an unhappy birth back in 1948. Ebert was at first to have produced the piece, then backed out; he was replaced by Ashton. However, in the event, it was such a great success that early disappointments were soon forgotten, and in later years Britten resented alterations to its original concept more than in any other case; indeed, Ashton's staging almost took on the aura of a tradition. Yet, paradoxically enough – Graham points out – much of the 'business' arranged by Ashton is not in the libretto but had been decided in consultation with Britten.

The difficulties over the television production of *Owen Wingrave* have been aired by Graham and others elsewhere. Graham himself was in the invidious position of watchdog over the television team, and in a sense he had to keep a watching brief for the composer, who was not always happy with what occurred. Yet, in defence of the television people, Graham points out that they made many concessions to the composer. They have to work to a certain format as there is so much material to produce, and in many respects they bent the rules to accommodate Britten, not least in agreeing to have the production shot at the Maltings. Britten's early fear that the work would not properly come to life until it was seen in the theatre may or may not be pertinent, but in the back of his mind was the thought that, in any case, the television production would have no more than two 'performances' and then be seen no more. Whatever the reason, when Graham eventually staged *Wingrave* at Covent Garden, the composer commented, '*Owen* has at last come home.' In view of the story, and Owen's relation to Paramore, that statement was somewhat ironic.

Graham, first as producer and then as one of the directors of the Aldeburgh Festival, saw much of Britten as an administrator. In working out programmes, and in the merely practical matter of balancing items, and making sure the orchestration worked throughout an evening, Britten was brilliant. His depth of knowledge of the whole repertory was extraordinary. He had many faithful and devoted souls to aid him, and from them he expected undivided loyalty. He needed that in order that his plans could be executed. Even if he was dealing with a distinguished guest, he would control the programme, often asking the artist to alter it to fit in with the shape of the festival. He always said that Aldeburgh should create everything and not take in ready-made articles in the way that Edinburgh was inclined to do. The stamp of artistic direction had to be on every event. As far as the music of Britten's contemporaries was concerned, Graham believes that there was no sense in which it was not adequately promoted – provided Britten liked the works – and he cites as proof the number of operas by other composers that were given over the years. On occasion, Britten would even have music performed that he did not necessarily admire.

He had a great knowledge of works that he did like. He knew the length and orchestration of most of the Beethoven and Brahms repertory; he knew Puccini's operas inside out. Indeed, from him he had learnt how to score quite heavily without obscuring the voices. His apprenticeship had been whole-hearted and thorough, and it showed when he came to writing his own works. Graham recalls a conversation between Britten and Shostakovich over Puccini's operas. Britten commented, 'Terrible operas.' Shostakovich corrected him, 'No, Ben – wonderful operas, but terrible music.' Britten admired Wagner but he considered the works often overblown, and he did not believe in composers writing their own librettos.

For a period, Graham was close to Britten personally, often staying at the Red House. That was before Graham became a director of the festival and moved to Suffolk himself. They often talked at length about their private lives and about their philosophy of life. Graham feels greatly indebted to all he learnt from the composer. Having come from a divided family, Graham had never had the benefit of fatherly advice. That he received from Britten; with his wisdom and concern for other people, he was a kind of surrogate parent. He was always ready with advice about Graham's career, but often liked to feel that Aldeburgh should come first. Inclinations in other directions were not always smiled on. That was particularly the case when Graham went to work at Glyndebourne. Such was the wound caused by the events of the late forties that Britten could hardly bear to contemplate a friend going there. John Christie's attitude had undoubtedly hurt the composer deeply.

When Graham moved to Suffolk he did not see Britten so frequently. He may indeed then have moved somewhat out of favour. Britten sometimes allowed what he considered slights to fester; he would not have it out with the person concerned, and that person often found out the composer's feelings too late to put the matter right. For instance, Britten was given to believe that the rehearsal schedule for *Wingrave* had been altered to serve Graham's convenience. Britten had imagined that Graham perhaps did not want to produce the opera. In fact, the whole thing had been totally misrepresented to Britten. Graham believes that he was never completely restored to favour after that. Certainly Britten's incipient illness might have had something to do with it, because he came to depend on, as it were, the lords and ladies of the bedchamber to keep others at bay. Graham points out that he sacrificed other engagements on many occasions to fit in with Aldeburgh plans; indeed he gave up an important Glyndebourne production in order to stage *Death in Venice*, after the date of the premiere of the Britten work was brought forward from September to June – a painful decision for Graham. Britten did acknowledge this, and expressed his gratitude accordingly. Britten also initially gave full support to the idea of the English Music Theatre, which was later so cruelly aborted by the Arts Council.

There was also the disappointment over the proposed *Anna Karenina*, originally conceived as an opera for Galina Vishnevskaya at the Bolshoi. Britten saw great difficulty in reducing the novel to libretto length, and asked Graham to attempt the task. They discussed the whole affair for three months at the Red House and Graham worked on it with the composer. He was never really happy with the text, and Britten was finally in a ferment. William Plomer was asked for his opinion of the libretto, and approved of Graham's approach, seeing no need for it to be rewritten. Plomer felt the text would be elevated by Britten's music. The Soviet invasion of Czechoslavakia put paid to any idea of a Bolshoi production and subsequent airing of the project in the press (as on a previous occasion) and the opera world in general was irritating.

Graham's disappointment over this work has to be set against all the years he worked with Britten on his major operas and the rapport they achieved in collaboration; Britten obviously relied on the confidence and competence of his producer in his later years with results that linger in the mind's eye. They were authentic in the best sense of the word.

21

Stephen Reiss

Stephen Reiss began his connection with Britten and Aldeburgh in a rather haphazard way. He had decided to settle in Aldeburgh after the Second World War in order to pursue his profession as a painter. In one of the early years of the festival, he was asked to run an exhibition because someone had let the organizers down. That was something of a success and Reiss was invited to join the festival's council.

At that time, Britten and Pears were somewhat dissatisfied with the way the festival was going. They were anxious to build a theatre to house opera, to overcome the inadequacies of the Jubilee Hall. They imagined that, with a bigger venue, receipts would be greater; but Reiss and others on the council pointed out that a larger place also meant larger overheads and expenses generally, and probably a bigger deficit. So in the end there would be a bigger economic problem than that already before them.

The good business sense shown by Reiss, though in some respects opposed to the founders' policy, was immediately perceived, and Reiss put forward further detailed ideas about how to make the festival viable. Basically, these concerned making some money – and then expanding. Gradually the festival did grow: the Jubilee Hall was enlarged, local churches were used, and popularity increased through the radio. Opera was still the heart of the festival; after all, as Reiss saw it, the festival had arisen out of the English Opera Group and the new works it gave were in a sense its *raison d'être*. Hence the need to improve facilities for opera.

By the time Reiss took over, he was lucky to find Britten and

Pears totally proficient in the running of the artistic side of the festival: they were already helped greatly by Imogen Holst. Although Reiss believes that the strategy was Britten's and the tactics Pears's, it was in the last resort Britten who was the more practical. For instance, Britten's own programmes were always at the heart of the planning, and were naturally the most popular events, so Britten would suggest that they should be performed midweek, because other events were just as likely to bring an audience at the weekend. Where the expense of an event or the numbers needed for a programme were concerned Britten was supreme. He was also tenacious in maintaining standards and originality in programmes, while Pears bubbled over with creative ideas.

Britten and Pears always involved themselves closely in the programme book. But, in administrative matters, they placed entire confidence in Reiss, who also managed the financial sides of the festival. Once the festival was on, Reiss attempted to protect Britten from the public importuning which had by then got out of hand; artists were always welcome at Crag House, then at the Red House, but not members of the public. For the latter the Festival Club was developed.

Britten demanded absolute loyalty from his colleagues. One factor was completely fatal to any artistic relationship, and that was if he discovered that anybody was talking about him behind his back. On one occasion a conductor was known to have made an unguarded remark. As soon as it reached Britten's ears, that conductor received his cards, although, like so many others, he was forgiven before the composer's death and invited back to the festival. Britten did not object to criticism made directly to him, but he could not tolerate any feeling that he was being the subject of gossip. There were even times, Reiss recalls, when he dried up as a composer because he felt that he was not properly appreciated, or that he was being betrayed in some way. During the preparation of *Noyes Fludde* in Orford Church, he got to hear of a faction in the village that was opposed to the piece, and this caused him such depression that he could not work for some two months after it. This kind of criticism was always magnified in his mind when he had not been present to witness the circumstances of the incident himself; and he might easily get a false idea of what had happened.

There were in the early days people in Aldeburgh itself opposed to the festival. That worried Britten very much, and Reiss considers that he personally did much to smooth relationships between town and festival by seeing that the right sections of the community received support through it. In that way people were won over to the festival's cause.

As is well known, Britten was very sensitive where criticism of his music was concerned. Reiss thinks he had good cause for this, since Britten often felt that where there *were* faults they had not been noticed, while better work was criticized for the wrong reasons. When he was bitter, it was only about unjust criticism, and old prejudices about writers died hard.

When Britten had decided on an objective, he was absolutely determined to achieve it. The enormous success of *Noyes Fludde* induced him to transfer the whole production to Southwark Cathedral in London. That was done against Reiss's better judgement but with Britten's usual ability for making miracles happen. The cost was, of course, huge. Similarly, Britten was adamant that *A Midsummer Night's Dream* (which is dedicated to Stephen Reiss) should be seen further abroad – and it was, again at great expense. By this time Reiss was aware that, while he had made the festival financially viable, the English Opera Group needed other resources. So he was greatly relieved when Covent Garden took the company under its wing.

Reiss had, as mentioned, succeeded in enlarging the Jubilee Hall to make possible the production of the *Dream*. Reiss saw this as a special performing centre for the festival; but Britten viewed it in somewhat grander terms and it was proposed to make it into a big arts centre. This brought about Reiss's undoing. Britten felt, particularly after the fire and the re-building, that the Maltings was not being sufficiently exploited, but he did not think that Reiss could cope with a whole new complex on his own. Unwisely, as he now views it, Reiss let it be known that he thought Britten wanted to move too fast, that a period of consolidation was needed, particularly as regards their ability to mount opera on a scale at least equal to that in the past.

Reiss's opinions were filtered back to Britten who was not unaware of Reiss's attitudes but felt he should have made his strong opinions known directly. Britten's hypersensitivity about people talking behind his back surfaced again. Reiss believes that this sensitivity arose from a basic insecurity, which was the result of his having adopted an unconventional life-style in the context of an exceptionally conventional upbringing and fundamental adherence to traditional moral values.

The mutual friends who told Britten of Reiss's views may not have appreciated Britten's sensitivity; they may even have felt that they were doing Reiss a service in trying to enlist Britten's sympathies for all the difficulties Reiss was then having. In doing so, they probably exaggerated or misrepresented him. In any case, Britten and Pears never openly discussed the coming rift. The actual break came over an apparently paltry matter of internal organization at the Maltings, but it so incensd Britten and Pears that they threatened to withdraw from the festival. This was the signal for Reiss to resign, which he did just after the 1971 festival.

There was another aspect to the affair. Britten undoubtedly believed that the artistic world ought to come to his support in financial terms. He believed, quite rightly, that he had something unique to offer, but that it was not his job to promulgate it. So he was sometimes reluctant to help or to make the right sort of noises to gain the needed money, and upset people unnecessarily. The approach to the Gulbenkian Foundation was a case in point. The attitude that the artist was in any way an ancillary operation in life was anathema to Britten; this was an arrogance of his – not personal but springing from his loyalty to the arts. Britten always felt that the arts must be properly recognized; anyone who thought otherwise was despicable. He would not on any occasion appear subservient to, or attempt to woo, those who held the purse strings, in order to get the cash. He was proud in the cause of music. And who's to say he was wrong?

Reiss was, over a long period, a close personal friend of the composer. He and his wife Beth went on four holidays with

Britten and Pears. As a travelling companion, Britten was very thoughtful and imaginative. He was passionately interested in what anybody was doing, as long as they were serious. He had a particular love of young people, because he thought they were straightforward and dedicated. He adored enthusiasm and whole-heartedness. He was fascinated by architecture, and indeed all forms of visual art. He was delighted by old films, being devoted to Chaplin, Laurel and Hardy, Garbo, Hitchcock and so on, as well as films of Russian opera and the Russian *Hamlet*. He was not interested in business or the City.

Their holidays together were to the Dordogne, to Germany and Denmark, to Wales, to the Borders; Britten usually drove his old Alvis, and always marvelled at the beauty of the countryside.

At home his timetable was rigorous. There were periods when he worked and he was not to be disturbed, and periods for recreation. Reiss fitted in with Britten's timetable. The composer showed interest in all the details of programming, the enlargement of Jubilee Hall, the building of the Maltings; progress reports were always welcomed, and he would help overcome any problem. Pears naturally did the same.

Their close working and personal relationships made the break, when it came, the more sad for all concerned. Perhaps Reiss had grown too close to the Red House and taken too much for granted, and he now regrets this. He also reflects that maybe he had become stale in some ways and it was time for a change, but the way the break came about still pains him. Later, there were attempts at reconciliation, but Reiss's feeling of betrayal made that hard. He feared that any meeting thereafter might be too emotional for anyone's good. You were either in or out – and Reiss could not forget that he was now 'out'; he also found it hard to accept that, after so many shared experiences, he was no longer part of the charmed circle. Reiss very much wanted a reconciliation. So, probably, did Britten; but his illness prevented it because he was not allowed to become excited. For all that, Reiss remains ever grateful for the benefits he gained from his friendship and work with such a great man.

Reiss's final reflections concern Britten's musicality and gifts on the platform. 'There was a complete absence of dogma in Britten's thinking, and he had a dogged practicality. Everything had to be freshly thought out and felt. His control was incredible: if, say, a platform had been so constructed that he had to sit at a harpsichord as if on the edge of a precipice, you knew he would be safe. Although he had total concentration on the music in hand, he never missed anything that was happening beside him; as a conductor, he was instantly aware of anything that might be amiss, yet in correcting it he was never dictatorial, always direct and kind. His players adored him. When the television film of *Billy Budd* was shown at the Aldeburgh cinema, the music had hardly begun before he noted that the sound track was marginally flat. Musicality ran in his veins; his reactions were instantaneous. Similarly, as soon as he heard the Maltings had burnt down, he did not dwell on lamentation but at once began planning how it could be rebuilt. His will was of iron. At the last, when he realized he had to adjust to his permanent frailty, his resolution was complete and unqualified. He was, in a word, extraordinary.'

22

Donald Mitchell

Donald Mitchell first met Britten when he was asked to edit the programme book for the 1958 Aldeburgh Festival, although he had been in correspondence with the composer earlier than that, when he and Hans Keller (q.v.) had edited their influential symposium on Britten in 1952. That book was in no way influenced by personal contact with the composer: Keller and Mitchell compiled it out of their enthusiasm for his music. After the book appeared, Britten wrote the editors a kind and appreciative letter. That led, some years later, to the invitation to Mitchell to work on the programme book.

From 1959, Mitchell was working as a music critic on the *Daily Telegraph*. At one point he had persuaded Britten to give him an interview for the newspaper – but at the last moment the composer, always reluctant to speak to the press, called off the appointment. 'I don't recall what excuse he made, but I remember thinking in later years that he couldn't face talking even with someone he knew to be sympathetic towards him and his work.'

While still with the *Telegraph*, Mitchell acted as adviser to Boosey and Hawkes, then Britten's publishers, on their music-publishing policy, particularly as regards the acquisition of new composers. At the same time he tried to keep an eye on Britten's affairs. Britten had become increasingly unhappy, as is common knowledge, with his relationship to his first publishers – Ralph Hawkes and Erwin Stein were no longer alive to encourage him and Anthony Gishford had been sacked. With hindsight, Mitchell feels that it was naive of him to think he could have succeeded in a task fraught with historical difficulties.

The connection with Boosey and Hawkes came to an abrupt end. But Mitchell was already advising Faber and Faber about their books on music and, in 1963, was involved in the firm's publication of a tribute to Britten on his fiftieth birthday, edited by Anthony Gishford, to which Mitchell contributed a notable essay on *Così fan tutte*. At that time, Faber was not publishing music. However, Britten, when looking later for a new publisher, approached the firm to ask if they would consider publishing his music, as he was not eager to consider moving to a firm abroad. The suggestion came in a memorable letter from Venice (where Britten was working on *Curlew River*), which led to Mitchell, somewhat unexpectedly, assuming the role of Britten's publisher.

Mitchell comments, 'I think this illustrates the importance he always attached to the *personal* link. He felt that to be crucial throughout his life. He wasn't impressed by abstract entities, however distinguished. He was not interested in a famous publishing house as such – he was quite prepared to make the break with a pretty famous one – but he felt that he needed the personal attention he hoped he would get at Faber. This insistence on personal relationships sometimes created difficulties: after all, personalities are sometimes more unstable or productive of disappointment than institutions.'

From the day Faber Music was created in 1963, Mitchell worked in close association with the composer – a happy professional and private relationship. 'Ben believed it was essential for a composer to have a creative connection with his publisher. He didn't, of course, need advice about *what* or *how* to write, not at this mature stage in his career; but he believed in a genuine dialogue. In the case of young composers he believed the advice and encouragement of a good publisher were vital – what he had in fact received himself from Ralph Hawkes. In his own case, he was most anxious that his affairs should be handled with tact and sensitivity. He abhorred the idea that everything had to be considered on a commercial or accountancy basis, although at the same time he was the most level-headed and business-like of men.

'That was his general idea about publishing and he placed great emphasis on it. He was just as keen that younger composers should benefit from such a constructive association as himself. On the more technical side of music publishing, of which I knew nothing when we embarked on setting up Faber Music, he was extremely demanding: he had a passion, from which I learnt much, for maximum clarity in the notation of musical sounds on the printed page. They had to be as clear and as practical as possible. After all, he took enormous pains to get everything precisely right himself, and he expected others to be no less thorough and painstaking. I spent many hours discussing with him the best way to lay out a page of music. I think we succeeded in meeting his challenging demands, which also helped, I believe, to advance the design of printed music in this country.'

Mitchell considers that the creation of Faber Music is illustrative of the way Britten liked to set up an environment and context sympathetic to himself, as he did when he started the Aldeburgh Festival, or later when he built the Maltings concert hall. The new publishing house, likewise, created the ideal circumstances for the publication of his music. 'That aspect of his achievement was part and parcel of his strong personality. He was determined to have the most appropriate environment in which to function. It was a desire that extended far beyond the desk at which he created his works. That was, to me, a fascinating side of him.

'Functioning as a composer was his whole world, even though he could be a very sociable person with his intimate associates when he was not working. The seemingly ruthless attitude towards some colleagues was caused by the demands he was making on himself in the cause of getting his music written. The creativity had to come first. Moreover, particular people were needed at particular times – and not at others. This, I think, was at the root of some unhappiness. Everyone, including himself, had to be sacrificed to the creative act. Also, people tended to forget just how busy he was, how concentrated was his life. Every minute of the day was consumed in some way. Demands on himself were easily double the demands he made on other people.'

Mitchell has learnt from his recent research that Britten wrote often with great difficulty, especially in his youth and early adulthood. That is indicated in his diaries from the thirties. Everything was scrutinized with the utmost care and very often rejected or rewritten several times. The seeming facility with which he composed was largely a public illusion. Nobody was more critical of his work than the composer himself. The extraordinarily elaborate procedure of selecting and testing, although somewhat fined down in later years, when it was a mental rather than a manuscript process, went on until the end of his life.

When Britten had completed a new work, he might ring up Donald Mitchell and ask him to come to hear a private play-through at the piano. 'In the case of *Death in Venice*, the experience was unforgettable. He played the whole work from start to finish from his pencil composition sketch, singing all the roles and knocking out the percussion parts on the piano rest. In many ways, it was the performance of the work I shall retain most vividly in my memory. Everything that was to make such a vivid impression when I heard it in the theatre was already present in his half-croaked performance, accompanied as it was by that magical piano playing which evoked the sounds of an orchestra. I heard all those extraordinary instrumental effects made mysteriously articulate at the keyboard.

'On these occasions he was always anxious to know what one thought. A sympathetic response was important for him. It was certainly rare for him to ask if anything was amiss or might be improved, at least of me. Indeed, the only occasion I can remember that happening was in connection with *Death in Venice*, because it had had to be rehearsed and performed without his being there to oversee it.'

Mitchell believes that, where critics were concerned, Britten had a low opinion of writers in newpapers, whom he considered to show a pretty poor standard of competence. He had never found criticism helpful. Writers who offered scathing reviews did not seem to him to be helping the cause of music in any way. It was a view that reflected the hurt done him as a young man, when he had so often been put down by the critics. Most of what had been written was unhelpful to his development, whereas he would have welcomed sympathetic and constructive criticism.

'That's why, I think, he so much welcomed that old book of mine and Hans Keller's. Even so, he seldom commented on what I had written. Just once in a while he might say something like, "Well, you really understood what that piece was about." I only mention this because it shows that even his response to positive criticism was not exactly enthusiastic. In a sense, the more searching it was, the more nervous he became.'

He hated verbalizing about any music, because he could not see the need for it. 'He felt that a work either communicated with an audience or it did not – if the latter, he felt that he'd failed in his job. That was the end of the story. Analysis meant very little to him. Indeed, I think he deeply distrusted it. I think he considered it positively dangerous to tinker about – to intrude – in areas that should be wholly the composer's concern, his unconscious creative processes. That was one reason he was so suspicious of the "new" music, especially when he noticed that digesting the explanations and programme notes often required more time and concentration than the work itself. All that was foreign to him, which doesn't mean that his own method of thinking and composing was in any way simple or facile – quite the contrary: it was as complex as that of any contemporary. He just didn't talk about it all the time.'

Having been such a close personal friend of the composer's during his latter years, Mitchell continues to miss his physical presence intensely. He and his wife found Britten a fascinating person to be with, not in the sense that afterwards Mitchell ran to his desk to write down some *bon mot*, but because his whole sensibility was so remarkable. 'One was aware of being with an extraordinarily endowed person. There was an exceptional spirit in him that made being with him inspiring. He was fundamentally a very serious person, but also great fun. He had a tremendous sense of humour, which added another dimension to one's relationship with him. He wouldn't have liked to be thought of as a saint – nor was he one – but he was an extremely kind and good man. It was rare for me to hear him say things about others which were lacking in charity; the thoughts may have been there, but silence was more often than not his form of criticism. He was much loved by all those who worked with him simply because he was so dedicated himself.

Because of that, one also became dedicated to his ideals. I'm sure performers felt that as much as anybody.

'He could be stubborn or unyielding, but I never found him unreasonable. He had a very powerful will, but then he needed that to accomplish what he did accomplish. One had to find a way of working with that. It was no use confronting Ben with a blank contradiction of what he wanted. Then you would encounter his determination to have his own way. But there were ways of giving him advice. If it was expressed as an alternative – not as opposition – he would often see his way to changing his mind. Others may not have understood that. He was invariably reasonable and practical. If persuaded to recognize a difficulty, he would help find a way of overcoming it.'

He remained an idealist to the end. 'In the early days, his convictions may have been expressed through the rather hectic left-wing politics of the 1930s. In later years, these were transformed into the larger ideals of pacifism, compassion, a desire to serve the community. He lived entirely for his music. If he was unhappy towards the end of his life, it was only because his disability prevented him from writing music. We should be grateful – as I think he was – that, when he was no longer able to write music, he died.'

He still had many ideas in mind: the unwritten works. There was to be a complementary piece to the *Spring Symphony*, a large choral and orchestral work built round poems concerned with the sea. Britten had thought a great deal about it, and had already chosen the poems he wished to set. The other big, unrealized project was a sequence of Christmas pageants, representing the stages in the Christmas story, to be performed successively and culminating, on the last night, in the birth of Christ. He had already devised a libretto, using the Chester Miracle Plays as his source, and formulated one or two musical ideas. The thought of taking on such a big project proved beyond his strength. He was also intrigued by the idea of writing music for a film of *The Tempest*, to be shot on Bali, with John Gielgud as Prospero. Preliminary conversations for this took place with Richard Attenborough. 'All these projects fell by the wayside because of his illness.'

23
Dame Janet Baker

Janet Baker, who sang so many memorable performances in concert and opera under Britten's musical direction, keeps a very special place in her memory for him and for her appearances at the Aldeburgh Festival. 'There certainly was an aura about him. I would compare it with working with someone like Klemperer. There was something special that made you give of your best.'

Her first appearance at Aldeburgh was in 1959 when she sang Berkeley's *Poems of St Teresa of Avila* at Blythburgh Church. 'I came totally under his spell from the beginning. I was amazed at his immediate grasp of the music in hand. At the same time, I remember he made a great effort to put me at my ease. I don't think he quite succeeded simply because to be with him was a bit like being with the Queen: in those circumstances you're never quite natural. I suppose it's almost like the sensation of being in love. Something happens to time, and one seems to be living in a highly volatile present. Nothing matters except the other person and the moments you spend with them. Just because you're in that state, all other experiences seem heightened.'

That kind of feeling naturally affected her performances with Britten. 'They had a special electricity, a magic allied to a performing ability at the very highest level. It was almost as if one was in the presence of Mozart or Schubert.'

He never played for any of her recitals, but she often took part in ensemble programmes of works such as Brahms's *Liebeslieder Walzer*. When Britten came to play for her solos, there was an undoubted frisson of excitement. 'I would compare it to working with artists such as Previn and Barenboim. Like them, Britten thought of the music in broad shapes. As an artist working in just one field, it's very stimulating to collaborate with someone like Britten, who worked in so many. A singer's approach to a piece is almost bound to be vertical, controlled by bar lines and vocal lines: that's the way we're taught to approach it. Britten, like Previn and Barenboim, was able to make you see the larger picture. That in no way lessens the approach of the accompanist *per se*, from whom other things can be learnt. It's simply a different experience.'

When Britten came to write *Phaedra* for her, she was surprised as she never expected him to compose specifically with her in mind. 'It's true that he had written pieces for Vishnevskaya and Fischer-Dieskau, but one was a great personal friend, the other a distinguished singer from abroad. Besides, I think a composer has to wait until a poem or whatever sparks off an idea that seems right for a particular voice or person. I think Ben had watched me grow as an artist over the years. Then, at the right time, he was ready to write something for me. The moment came when he heard me sing *Nuits d'été*: that may have convinced him that I'd gone beyond what I had previously been able to manage.

'When *Phaedra* arrived, I was overwhelmed by its passion and feeling. Even more awesome was to collaborate with the composer on it, to create the interpretation in his presence. That moment is mine for ever.'

There were many other times when he was perceptive in leading her towards the right interpretation, or when he judged what was good for her voice and personality. 'Lucretia had been written for Kathleen Ferrier. For a long time Ben seemed unwilling for me to sing it. My voice was not as low-lying as hers, and he was afraid that it might be hard for me to encompass some of the tessitura. When I did eventually undertake it, I think he was pleased. I found it profoundly satisfying.'

With Kate Wingrave, written for her, the problem was different. The character was uncongenial, and Britten could feel that portraying such a hateful person was beginning to affect the singer. 'He was so amazingly sensitive to such vibrations that he came over to me at rehearsal and said something that calmed my nerves; he knew instinctively what I was going through.'

On another occasion, she was working with him on the *Spring Symphony*. 'I was experiencing some difficulty with my solo, "Out on the Lawn". He immediately realized the problem, and assured me all would be well on the night – as indeed it was – and he then conveyed his gratitude in a single glance. It was typical of his understanding.'

In the case of *Albert Herring*, she learnt from him that in playing comedy one must not find the humour amusing oneself, that the characters were not in the least funny or eccentric to themselves – which is exactly why the audience thinks them so. 'It used to drive him mad to see performances of this opera in Germany, where the singers would ham up the characters unmercifully. That destroyed the whole point of the work.'

Where technical matters were concerned, he left singers to themselves. 'He gave artists the framework in which to work out their vocal problems. Whatever the music, one knew with him that the tempo would be ideal. Operating within that framework, one was well on the way to giving a definitive account of the work in hand. He would spend time commenting or enlarging on performing points and that made one feel very close to him, even if he wasn't there in person.'

She never presumed on their relationship. As she appreciates solitude, she could see that Britten did the same. 'But I knew that, if the need had arisen, I could have turned to him for advice. I think that was implicit in our understanding of each other. There was genuine affection on both sides, but I realized that it would be wrong to take too much from someone whose main purpose in life was to spend as much time as possible writing music. While one was with him, he gave one his all, but it was incumbent on the performer not to ask for more. As a busy artist myself, I know that there must be time to recuperate.'

She was fully aware of his so-called dark side. There could be pain and sorrow, though she did not experience it, perhaps because she realized that it was sensible not to get too near the sun for fear of being burnt. 'If you worked too closely with a man like him, you could face the prospect of being taken over completely. I think he was quite entitled to take what he needed from others. It might seem like ruthlessness, but success in life sometimes *requires* ruthlessness. He did not want to hurt anyone, but the task in hand was more important than anything or anybody. Besides, he was a very attractive personality who drew people to him like moths to a flame. He had to protect himself against them or else he would have no time left to compose.

'From those who worked with him he demanded absolute loyalty. The commitment had to be complete. If anybody fell below his high standards, they were asking for trouble. To blame him for that is probably unfair.'

For those who remained loyal, to return to Aldeburgh was like 'going home'. Dame Janet still feels like that about the place even though Britten is no longer physically present. It is part of her life and will remain so. 'Aldeburgh is closely woven into what I have done, what I am, and that's something not to be lightly cast off, even when the central person around whom it revolved has gone. When those who have no memory of him take over, then Aldeburgh will undoubtedly move in another direction. The time of the festival is sacrosanct in my diary; even if other engagements have been planned much further ahead, most years I keep a place in June to be filled in by Aldeburgh. I owe it to Ben's memory and to all the kindness he showed to me.'

24
Keith Grant

When Keith Grant took up his post as manager of the Covent Garden Opera Company, as it was then known, it had just been expanded to include that of general manager of the EOG, which had come under the Royal Opera House's aegis a year earlier. He had immediately to develop the relationship between the opera company and Britten. David Webster, then Covent Garden's general administrator, left Grant in no doubt about what difficulties there might be in the new connection. There had been lengthy discussion as to whether the EOG should come under the custodianship of Covent Garden or Sadler's Wells, partly because relations between Britten and Webster had been, as Grant says, uncertain at best. Indeed it was John Tooley, then assistant general administrator, who was largely responsible for building up trust between the composer and the Royal Opera House. Grant's first task in his new post was arranging performances of *Dido and Aeneas* at Drottningholm, Aldeburgh and the City of London Festivals, most of them conducted by Britten, with Janet Baker as Dido, her first assignment with the EOG. Immediately, he was thrown into contact with Britten – just three weeks after his appointment to his new post. Britten proved kind and considerate towards Grant, who had no previous experience of running an opera company and who was now taking seventy people on a tour of Sweden. They immediately created a working relationship. Although not close friends, they always got on well together, respecting each other's professional skills.

Britten was not an easy master, but his organizational ability was enormous; he had an ice-cool mental composure. He could at once see what the administrative problems would be arising out of a given decision. Just as he could keep large orchestral concepts in his head, so he could retain a great deal of mundane detail. On the other hand, he could easily and deliberately overlook such matters if he wanted to, or if he wanted to goad a person to make renewed efforts to overcome a difficulty.

He was always adept at resolving any artistic conflict. If there was some problem over the clashes of engagements of a singer, he would sort it out with great care so that as far as possible, he would end up with the cast he wanted. In other words, Grant found him a tough taskmaster not because of any personality clash but because he was so quick-witted that he could easily 'out-perform' the manager if the manager wasn't careful. Therefore Grant had at all times to be on his toes. This was another of Britten's immense gifts: he was master of whatever he set his mind to. If the occasion had required it, he could have managed an opera company better than anyone.

Where casting was concerned he had meticulously high standards. He also had very particular likes and dislikes of various singers. Some might be good executants of his music, but they might not be acceptable in other ways. Indeed he would work only with people in whom he had total confidence. That could produce problems with a company like the EOG that had no permanent base and was not in existence throughout the year. Nor was the availability of the finance needed for its programmes established sufficiently in advance for the group to be able to book the artists Britten wanted. Artists might wait for his call – for he had great pull over them – but they had to bear in mind more definite engagements.

In addition, the choice of cast had to be agreed not only with Britten but also with Pears and the conductor of the day. And it often took time for a consensus to emerge. The ultimate decisions were usually sound but they could provoke nail-biting crises.

Grant had a chance to observe Britten's work in detail during the EOG's tour of Russia in 1964. At that point Britten was at the height of his fame in the Soviet Union. By dint of successful records and close relationships with certain Soviet artists, he was amazingly popular there, so he set great store by the tour, and felt that to an extent his reputation could suffer if it did not go well. He was peculiarly solicitous about the repertory, the casting, the venues, and the detailed conditions. Of course, the Soviet authorities wanted him to conduct everything and Pears to sing in all the operas, and together they did a tremendous number of performances – no less than thirty-two in twenty-nine days, in three different cities. Britten conducted more than half. The company of sixty were under severe strain, particularly as fourteen out of some thirty singers fell ill. Flu was rampant.

In the expected crises, Britten was a tower of strength. Besides his performing duties, he took part in many interviews and press conferences, where he had to answer frequent questions about the Beatles, usually commenting that he wished they would get beyond a guitar as accompanying instrument. He was vexatious about ill-informed interviewers, particularly on the occasion when they all went out to television headquarters on the Lenin Hills outside Moscow. In a car on the way to that fortress-like place, they were stopped by a security post who knew nothing of Britten or the interview. They were forced out of their limousine by two formidable armed ladies and into a bare brick hut because they did not have the right passes. Britten became more and more nervous, until they were eventually allowed in. During the interview Britten became increasingly frosty, because it proved perfunctory in the extreme. This lack of professionalism infuriated him. On these travels in Russia, Britten was obviously under strain and worried by the poor diet. But he was always all right on the night.

1964 was also the year of *Curlew River*, which marked a big departure in Britten's and the EOG's work. The melding of Eastern and monastic influences is well-known for its arresting effect. The dedication and tension brought to the piece by the singers and instrumentalists under Colin Graham's and Pears's influence has not been forgotten. At the time, though, Britten was very much aware that he might not be able to sell this new vision to the public. He had conviced his librettist, William

Plomer, and all concerned, but would it work? He also fretted about Pears's appearance in a female part. Very few English actors, let alone singers, managed this successfully. Then there was the technical problems of the orchestra playing without a conductor.

The première was put in further jeopardy by an electricity failure caused by a thunderstorm on the first night. The piece might have worked well by candlelight but for the fact that the organ was being powered by electricity; the audience had to be stood down for more than an hour. Grant went to see Britten with some trepidation; he felt sorry for the composer who had had so many tensions and then, almost literally, been struck by lightning. But, as so often, Britten's reaction was totally relaxed and he was able to laugh off this unfortunate act of God. All the nervousness had apparently gone from him, and in the event he enjoyed a triumph, in spite of all the problems.

Britten might say that he was not concerned about certain aspects of new productions because they were not his department, but Grant learnt by experience that woe betide him if Britten was not consulted about every detail. Britten wanted total control.

In the case of *Death in Venice*, Grant's impression was that, unlike on some earlier occasions, Britten had supreme confidence that he could bring off the work. He was given confidence by having all his friends round him: the Pipers (q.v.), Frederick Ashton (q.v.), Steuart Bedford (q.v.), Colin Graham (q.v.), John Shirley-Quirk, Deanne Bergsma (Mrs Grant), and Pears, who bore the brunt of the composer's worries about the opera, of course. That confidence was totally justified.

During Grant's period with the EOG, many operas were produced with singers other than the creators in many of the roles. Although Britten was not always happy with the results, he grew reconciled to differing interpretations, except perhaps in the case of Pears's roles, where he was bound always to hear his friend's voice, technique and interpretative powers, simply because the parts had been written with Pears's attributes in mind. Britten might admire the alternatives but he could hardly be expected to relish them. When another tenor sang

Albert Herring in Russia, Grant recalls Britten's saying to Pears, 'Peter, I wish you could sing the role again.' In a similar way he would sometimes have nostalgia for another creator – such as Jennifer Vyvyan as the governess in *The Turn of the Screw*.

Over the years Grant inevitably saw the ruthless element in the composer's make-up, the occasions on which he lost confidence in a singer or player and made their life hard. Confidence once lost was hardly ever restored. Grant had to be the buffer between Britten and the artist, whom Grant had engaged. Grant thinks these losses of confidence were the result of the punishing standards Britten set himself. The composer reckoned that the degree of preparation he himself made before a performance should be equalled by the other artists. If they came unprepared to rehearsal, his faith in them evaporated at once. There was hardly any allowance made for advancing years, or even illness; he had a standard that, with very few exceptions, he insisted should be maintained. 'Old time's sake' or any other such concepts did not play any part in his thoughts. If he applied such judgements, he stood by them, even if in personal terms because of his basic kindnesss, they cost him much heartache; his private friendships had to be weighed against his professional drive: if one had to go, it was the friendship.

A facet of Britten's character that Grant considers has been under-emphasized is his sense of humour. In spite of the pressure on him to play the great man, and the essential melancholy of his nature, Britten could be very humorous in conversation. He did not tell jokes, but had a good line in quick repartee and was one of the most agreeable after-dinner companions that could be imagined. The memory of the sheer enjoyment of his company will always remain with Grant. What Keith Grant recalls above all from his happy years with the EOG is the excitement generated by the creation of new works in the composer's presence; this excitement is hard to recapture in words, but it lives on vividly in the memory of those who took part in the creation. There was not merely the growing expectancy felt at rehearsals, but also the hours of talk at the Red House and at Britten's flat in London about every aspect of production. To watch someone who had so many creative ideas and whom it was difficult to imagine making a wrong decison in artistic terms was a experience not to be forgotten. There were so many ideas thrown up that, sadly, never came to fruition, particularly as regards stagings of Mozart's operas. Grant says without exaggeration that the man's gifts were unparallelled.

Since he worked so closely on the operas, Grant's choice of favourite works is interesting. He is passionately enthusiastic about *Curlew River* and *Death in Venice* (even though he has doubts about the Games of Apollo and its staging). As for *The Turn of the Screw*, so much admired by others, Grant finds it has some of Britten's most ravishing music and believes the libretto is a consummate work of art, but there is some atmosphere in it that he finds problematical – and, interestingly enough, this work was not a success in Russia, partly because of difficulties in comprehending the ghosts.

25

Mstislav Rostropovitch

Rostropovich first met Britten in 1960, in the green room at the Royal Festival Hall, London, when Britten and Shostakovich were sharing a box to listen to the cellist playing the latter's first cello concerto. Britten was nothing like Rostropovich expected; in his mind's eye he had visualized a large and imposing figure. The reality was somewhat confusing but, once he regained his composure, the cellist asked Britten whether he would write a cello piece for him – as that had been his one dream.

In a sense, this was the end of a chain reaction that had begun in 1949, when the composer Myaskovsky wrote a sonata for Rostropovich. Rostropovich played it at a performance at which Prokofiev was present and immediately Prokofiev agreed to write a work for him. At the premiere of Prokofiev's *Sinfonia Concertante*, Shostakovich, who was in the audience, decided to write his concerto for Rostropovich. Now, it was Britten's turn to complete the chain.

The following day, Rostropovich told his fellow countryman Genadi Rozhdestvensky how overjoyed he was that Britten was to visit his hotel to discuss the proposed composition. A sonata was agreed upon – to the cellist's delight – on the sole condition that the first performance should be given at the Aldeburgh Festival. Rostropovich agreed, but in some trepidation because he was concerned about whether or not he would gain permission from the Soviet authorities to attend the festival. Britten sent the score, rather late, to the cellist in Moscow and, in order to run through and discuss the work, Rostropovich stopped off in London for a day on his way to South America. Both artists were somewhat inhibited at first but, after a couple of whiskies, they began to respond to each other. Indeed, at the end of each movement, they embraced heartily, such was the rapport that had been achieved.

At the end of the run-through, Britten said nothing. However, at lunch with Peter Pears later, Britten began to hum the second theme of the first movement in such a way that Rostropovich realized he had not been playing it quite to the composer's satisfaction. That was Britten's sole comment.

Even so, the premiere nearly did not take place. The Culture Ministry in Moscow felt that the fee being offered was not high enough and wanted to prevent Rostropovich from leaving for Aldeburgh when the time came. (Indeed, on a later occasion, he *was* prevented from coming, for the premiere of the third suite – an act for which he has still not forgiven the authorities in Moscow: nor incidentally has his wife Galina Vishnevskaya forgotten that she was prevented from singing at the *War Requiem*'s first performance in 1962.) The premiere of the sonata took place in 1961 in the Jubilee Hall and was an unforgettable experience for Rostropovich – and not only for musical reasons. It was also the contact with the composer that made it so memorable because Britten was such an inspiring personality. This was to be the start of a firm artistic and personal friendship. Rostropovich echoes the sentiments of the priest at Britten's funeral, who commented that all present should smile because they had had the privilege of knowing the composer.

There followed a succession of notable works for the cellist: the *Cello Symphony*, the three suites, and *The Poet's Echo* for Galina and Rostropovich (here as pianist). Rostropovich admires them all in their different ways, but he believes that the time for the *Cello Symphony* has not yet arrived. While the public has taken the *War Requiem* – a work Rostropovich has often conducted – to its heart, the *Cello Symphony* has to an extent been left to languish, although Rostropovich thinks that it is one of the most phenomenal works in the instrument's repertory. He believes that, once its complexity is understood, its day will come. As far as the suites are concerned, he considers each has its own particular idiom. A composer would have to be an amazing virtuoso to write with such variety for a single instrument.

The history of the genesis of those suites is quite amusing. After an appearance at Aldeburgh, Britten and Rostropovich had to travel to Rosehill in Cumberland for a recital. They drove there in Britten's old Alvis in the company of Pears and Marion Harewood (as she then was). The first night was spent at a hotel. For the second they were to stay at Harewood House, where for the first time in his life the cellist was to meet a real princess (Princess Mary, sister of George V, father of Lord Harewood). Until then princesses had been confined in his experience to fairy tales – they were distant beings to be approached by knights in shining armour. Such was the *idée fixe* in his mind that, when they were approaching Harewood House, Rostropovich jumped out of the car, pirouetted in the air and landed on his knees. The act was repeated frequently. Britten was a little worried about how his friend was going to behave in the presence of the princess. He told Rostropovich that his performance was perfect but that he should take into account the fact he was to meet a dignified and fragile old lady. If, on account of his behaviour, she should die of shock, there would be a scandal. However, Rostropovich was not to be denied: he felt that he had spent so much time perfecting his pirouette he must be able to use it at the appropriate moment. At Lincoln, over lunch, a further attempt was made to persuade the determined Rostropovich. Britten's final plea was couched in desperate terms. He said he would give his friend anything he wanted provided he refrained from his pirouette. Rostropovich immediately seized the menu and wrote on it:

> I, Benjamin Britten, promise to write six major works for cello in recompense for which Slava Rostropovich will agree not to perform his pirouette in front of Princess Mary.

Ben signed it – and the witnesses were Peter Pears and Marion Harewood. When they entered the Princess's presence, Rostropovich made a few jerky movements – just as a reminder of the agreement. Britten's word was kept to the extent of three pieces. Unfortunately, the menu with the agreement on it was left behind in Moscow when Rostropovich moved from his flat.

Of the suites, each of which has its own personality,

Rostropovich has a particular affection for the third – the sad one based on themes taken from Tchaikovsky's notebooks. It finishes with a liturgy from the church services: 'With the saints you will find your rest.' Even when he played it during Britten's lifetime, he found it hard to restrain himself from crying. Now that Britten is dead, Rostropovich finds it difficult to play it at all.

Rostropovich often stayed at the Red House with the composer and Pears. They were memorable days in his life, not only because of the music-making but because Britten had such a sense of humour. He recalls that Britten was quite unlike any other person he has ever known – the composer had such fine perception of other people's feelings, problems and pleasures. Whenever the cellist was going through a difficult time – even if he didn't realize it himself – Britten was quick to notice. When Rostropovich and his wife were in Edinburgh at the time of the Soviet invasion of Czechoslovakia (at the airport an old man shook his fist at them, saying, 'Go home'), they decided to stay in their hotel as much as possible. But Britten walked into their room and said he had come on purpose to take them to a rehearsal of the *Church Parables*. As Rostropovich puts it, he surrounded the harassed couple 'like a guardian angel'. It was a sign of real friendship and understanding. On another occasion, after Shostakovich's death was announced (and Rostropovich could no longer return to his country), Britten immediately understood his feelings: the first telegram Rostropovich received was from Britten and it was full of sympathy for what his friend must be suffering. As soon as it was announced that Rostropovich had been appointed music director of the Washington Symphony, Britten was asked to write a work for them. An oratorio was started but did not go beyond the first fourteen pages before Britten died. There may have been a difficulty over this work as suggested by Britten's comment that now he had to write for himself, for Rostropovich – and for Shostakovich.

Rostropovich praises, in glowing terms, Britten's perceptions and sensitivity; they went far beyond anything he has ever encountered in another musician. That, and his extraordinary understanding of other people, is what Rostropovich will always remember in his friend. He recalls communicating with Britten in the years before he (Rostropovich) could speak much English. He used to converse with Britten in poor German. Britten could speak that language much more fluently than Rostropovich, yet when they talked together at that time Britten as it were 'forgot' his German, so as to be on the same level as his friend. Indeed, in the end, the language came to be known as 'Aldeburgh Deutsch' (a 'language' that Marion Thorpe, whose mother tongue is German, could sometimes not understand!).

In preparing a new work of Britten's with the composer, very few corrections or alterations had to be made. In that, Rostropovitch recalls, he was on a par with Shostakovich. Both were so meticulous in their scoring that changes were minimal. Britten apparently wrote for the cello as if he had played the instrument himself. He even wrote passages that Rostropovich would have thought to be impossible on the instrument, but such was Britten's technical knowledge that they proved capable of execution. Perhaps it was the fact that Britten once played the viola that made him so adept at writing for the lower instrument. Similarly, he had an altogether exceptional ear for orchestration. That can be seen particularly in the *Cello Symphony*, of which Rostropovich gave the premiere in Moscow with the composer conducting. Although many found it puzzling, Rostropovich remembers that Gilels, who heard it on the radio, telephoned him later to way what a work of beauty he had found it. Richter, who was present at the British premiere in Blythburgh Church, also appreciated its significance in Britten's output.

For Rostropovich, Britten's music in general is characterized by its marked individuality, so that one can almost at once recognize a piece as being by him. The language is clear and very personal. He also believes that Britten's wonderfully human qualities are reflected in the music and the feeling for beauty is highly developed. Only in some passages in *Death in Venice* does one find the kind of anger, irony and tension found in so much of Shostakovich's work. Rostropovich thinks that it may have been Britten's fight against ill-health that gave his writing here an added will-power and force.

After the composer's death, Rostropovich felt it was his duty to accept the post as co-director of the Aldeburgh Festival – something he owed to the memory of his friend. It was partly because of Britten's admiration for Tchaikovsky that Rostropovich conducted, for instance, *Eugene Onegin* at Aldeburgh. Also, that production reflected Britten's concern to develop the talents of young people (the cast was of young professionals and the Snape-Maltings Training Orchestra took part, with which Rostropovich also gave an unforgettable reading of Tchaikovsky's *Serenade for Strings*).

Rostropovich's final thoughts on Britten return to the *War Requiem*. Shostakovich considered it the greatest work of the twentieth century and – going to the piano to play one of its main themes – Rostropovich recalled that Shostakovich regretted he had not thought of the idea himself. This work always has a magical effect on audiences: it is a positive reminder of what another war might entail. It is a fresh impression of war's horror – that is its greatness. It was, too, in a sense, a mirror of Britten's own personality, his concern for the individual's importance. Rostropovich acknowledges that Britten had his own personal problems – he lived in his own inner world – but he believes that these were expressed in his work. When he met you, Britten would smile and forget his own difficulties. In his music-making there was something special and unforgettable. Rostropovich can never play Schubert's *Arpeggione Sonata* again because his and Britten's performances together were unique experiences – one composer's understanding of another's. It was also a search for perfection. When they performed the Schumann concerto together, Britten would go on rehearsing until he achieved the performance he had in his mind's ear; as conductor, player, composer and friend, Britten was a singular sounding-board with an ear for sensitive perfection.

26

Robert Tear

Robert Tear first encountered Britten when singing under Imogen Holst as a member of her Purcell Singers. He remembers that they all looked up to Britten as a 'great old sage' in the background. If he spoke to you, you were lucky. Tear feels there was almost an aura of holiness round Britten, and that it was something much encouraged by the Aldeburgh circle. Here was a sort of god. One day Meredith Davies, who was then musical director of the English Opera Group, conducted a performance of *Messiah* in which Tear was a soloist, and Davies mentioned that the company was looking for singers to make the 1964 tour of the Soviet Union. Tear was asked to an audition attended by Britten, Pears, Davies and Colin Graham. He 'passed' on singing 'Tarquin's Ride' from *The Rape of Lucretia*. However, his first job for the company was not in Russia, but covering Pears as the Madwoman in *Curlew River* at the 1964 Aldeburgh Festival. He did not actually sing the part until the production reached Southwark Cathedral in London during the City of London Festival that summer. As most critics were otherwise engaged in the evening, they asked if they could attend the afternoon performance, at which Tear was to sing. Britten came round before it began. He astonished the tenor by saying he was using the role as a vocal exercise and that he was disappointed by Tear's approach to it – not the best prelude to what was to follow. However, Tear treated the off-putting remark as a great spur. Britten, Tear thinks, was perhaps being devastatingly waspish in order to throw out a challenge – if so, it worked. The composer probably believed that the difficult part seemed much too easy to the tenor; he wanted Tear to be acutely conscious of the meaning of every word that he was going to sing.

For the following ten years, Tear was a regular member of the EOG, seconding the Pears's parts, creating some of his own. But Tear feels that Britten would only allow someone to shine as long as it was not too brightly. If a singer's interpretations became too personal, or his ideas about a role too individual, he was in danger of overstepping the mark. Yet, against that were the remarks dropped by Britten which gave Tear new insights into what he was supposed to be doing: Britten never appeared to be directly coaching a singer, but he was always about at rehearsals listening and summing up performances. His comments at the end could be revelatory.

Tear's abiding memory of Britten is of his immense charm. He recalls that, when Britten spoke to him, he made him feel the most important person in the world. At that moment he seemed to care for the singer very intensely. Tear finds that it gave him a very strange feeling when someone as important as Britten sat with him alone and gave him his full attention. Their relationship extended to games of table tennis in the garage at the Red House, played by the composer with demon-like effect. On one occasion, Tear appeared to be winning, when Britten, with his fiendish spin services, leapt ahead and won. Britten looked at Tear quizzically, and said, 'One thing you must learn: you will never beat the composer!' These relaxed and friendly moments contrasted with the occasional cruelties – times when Tear wondered whether even the greatness of the music compensated for the pain caused.

Tear's break with the composer came in 1970 when he decided to accept the role of Dov in the premiere at Covent Garden of Tippett's *The Knot Garden* instead of taking the part of Lechmere in *Owen Wingrave*. Having never sung at Covent Garden, Tear thought he must accept the part of Dov. Besides, he had come to a point in his career when the somewhat oppressive influence of Britten and Aldeburgh was inhibiting his individuality. Britten considered this disloyal, and from then on Tear ceased to appear at Aldeburgh or with the EOG. Tear acknowledges that he was in a sense biting the hand that had fed him, but he thought that he could not continue simply to be a satellite. He had grown out of the ultra-refined atmosphere surrounding the composer.

He also wanted to bring his own interpretations to Britten's music, rather than those of Pears. His attitude to the music is more dramatic, more personal, than Pears's reflective one. Tear wished to give a greater immediacy to the text, a more subjective view.

As a performer, Britten was in a class of his own, Tear considers. He managed to give an artist great space in which to work, and yet maintain total control over a piece as a whole. The music was never hard-driven, yet it was always vivid and exciting. Britten persuaded the English Chamber Orchestra to play with a particular intensity that was all his own. His technique was far from perfect, but then it did not need to be because of his complete musicality. Tear found him pointillistic as a pianist – almost but not quite to the stage of being mannered – yet everything was absolutely clear and the ideas were well fed. In Mozart he was unsurpassed . . . symphony, concerto or choral works. In Bach, he never neglected the emotion, as do so many conductors today, but he did not allow the music to become sentimental in the old way. Britten found the happy medium. Had Britten been able to use old instruments, Tear thinks we would have had the ideal Bach – neither sterile and stone age nor overblown.

Tear observed the familiar dislike of Britten for Beethoven – 'silly old potato' is a description recalled – and Brahms. Britten thought Beethoven was unable to write a good tune and Brahms was too predictable. Wagner was also abhorred, at least at the time Tear knew the composer. Discussions often revealed Britten's love of Mahler, particularly his orchestration, and Mahler's influence is felt in *Nocturne*, which is dedicated to Alma Mahler.

Tear frankly admits that, while he was deeply involved in Aldeburgh, he found Britten's own music increasingly facile, but, since the composer's death, he has changed his mind considerably. The *War Requiem* was, at first, one of the pieces he found most contrived, and, after singing the work ten times on the trot in Israel, he found it thin, but more recently he has come to love it more.

Tear finds, of course, that the music for tenor is very much tailored to Pears's style, and he fears that, in the long run, other voices may not be able to cope with it. He thinks his own facility in that respect lies in the fact that in his formative years he deliberately modelled himself on Pears's style. The technique involved is almost wholly attuned to Britten's music and is difficult to use in other pieces. He believes that, 'if it is not sung in the Pears fashion, it will sound wrong-headed'. As an example of what he means, Tear cites Britten's own well-known adverse reaction to Jon Vickers's interpretation of Peter Grimes: he simply did not want to hear the music sounding in a different manner from that in which he had conceived it. Tear also points out that *Les Illuminations*, not written for Pears's voice, is much easier to sing, because the singer does not have a specific style superimposed on the reading.

Having said that, he considers that, paradoxically, Britten wrote in a masterly fashion for the voice: he never takes a singer too low or too high, never asks him to use difficult vowels.

Tear returns ultimately to the contradiction in Britten's character between kindness and ruthlessness, and his ability to share confidences with people, yet to search out uncannily their psychological weaknesses. These were traits people had to bear with as part of working with one of the great creative minds of our time – and it was worth it.

Letters confirm Britten's concern for Tear's career and also his acuteness in judging practical matters:

22 December 1966
I have delayed answering your letter of November 24th until we saw the results of the strenuous efforts of John Tooley and the Group to get the *War Requiem* in Lisbon shifted to June 4th. Now I hear that these have failed and as far as you and April [Cantelo] are concerned the thing has fallen through. I am sorry about this but I do feel very strongly that it would have been unwise for you and April to sing the *War Requiem* on the fifth, travel overnight down to Aldeburgh and then have the full orchestral rehearsal on the sixth, then on the seventh the first performance of the opera [*A Midsummer Night's Dream*] in the

festival, the first theatrical programme in the new hall [The Maltings] ever and possibly your first performance of such a heavy role. I am sure you *could* have managed it – that is one of the advantages (?) of modern travel – but I think it is a temptation a singer, especially a young one, should resist. This kind of rushed life is one of the curses of life today, a kind of greed to do everything that is physically possible, but it lowers standards and harms artists in a sad way. It is important that your Lysander should do you and the work justice, but these circumstances would have made it difficult for you to give that little extra something that a part like this demands. It would also have come out of any ensemble rehearsals prior to the dress. I know that you will be disappointed about not doing this performance, but you will I know have very many opportunities to do splendid performances of the role, and since I am highly interested in the development of your career, which has started so brilliantly, I'm sure this present course is the wisest one.

PS I do hope that you are pleased with the wonderful reaction to your Novice in *Billy Budd* on TV, a splendid and touching performance.

13 July 1969
So sorry about the chicken pox. You must have been feeling rotten, and it was noble of you to go through with the tour. I do see your point about Arbace in [*Idomeneo*], but I have never considered doing away with the aria. The part as you have developed it, adding the High Priest to it, for instance, simply must have a statement of some kind. I quite understand your problem about being an 'elder statesman' at your age, but then lots of parts you do, and will do, aren't precisely 'type-casting', to name only the Tempter and Todd in Gordon Crosse's [*The Grace of Todd*]. It is a matter of thinking yourself into the part as you do so brilliantly. But before you commit yourself for next year, let's have a long talk about it; perhaps during the TV session for *Idomeneo* there'll be time. In the meantime warmest congratulations for what you have already done with 'old' Arbace.

Tear remembers that Britten never failed to answer letters promptly. That was part of his concern for other people and his generally fastidious method of working.

27

Graham Johnson

Graham Johnson, the youngest contributor to these memoirs, first came into contact with Britten in 1970, when he was still a student at the Royal Academy of Music. He had got to know the composer's music a couple of years earlier, when he came to England from Africa, and fell under the spell of the operas and song cycles. Having written the composer a fan letter, detailing what the music meant to him, he received a handwritten letter from Britten by return of post, saying that he was at that moment very busy with the festival but perhaps they could meet later. As Johnson was soon to gather, his getting a letter from the Red House was like a young musician of Wagner's day receiving a letter from Wahnfried.

The following year, Johnson went to Aldeburgh for the festival, and Britten somehow found time to see him. They had half an hour together. At that time, Johnson had in mind to be a composer himself, and Britten agreed to see some of his music. There must have been many other such visitors. Johnson recalls picking up a couple of pine cones outside the Red House, and giving one to a girl who was as awestruck with Britten's music as he was. He believes that it is natural and good for a young musician to feel such reverence: here was a composer of unquestionable genius producing and playing music in a unique way of which young musicians could actually be a part; they could adopt him as a real idol – not that Britten encouraged this.

A year later, Johnson was organizing a concert at the RAM to celebrate Alan Bush's seventieth birthday. He wrote to Peter Pears asking if he would take part. The tenor replied in the affirmative and agreed to sing Bush's finest cycle, *The Voices of the Prophets*. When Johnson met him, Pears said, very charmingly, 'The composer of the *Serenade* sends his greetings.' Johnson was astounded that he should be remembered in that way. The day after the Bush concert, Johnson was invited to lunch with Britten and Pears at their London home, from which followed invitations to the Red House. Johnson, at that time, had no relatives in London, so the hospitality and kindness was more than welcome. At the lunch Johnson recalls saying to Britten, rather naively, that he was very nervous about a concert he was to take part in that evening at the RAM, and commenting how wonderful it must be to be famous and not have to be nervous. Britten replied, 'You're quite wrong; it gets much worse the more famous you become – you have to prove yourself from the very first note.'

Yet Johnson recalls that, when Britten came on to the platform to play, he gave an impression of total stillness. 'He took his glasses out of his pocket. His hands went to the keyboard. From that moment on, he seemed utterly prepared. There was no extraneous movement. Those marvellous hands of his then seemed to encompass everything under them, including a tendency that he had inherited from being a viola player to do vibratos on the piano. The most magical effect seemed transmitted from brain to fingers without any changes in posture, so that the total impression was of someone with almost incredible self-possession. You would never have been aware that he almost had to be pushed on to the stage, such were his pre-concert nerves.'

However, Britten was often self-deprecating about his playing. Johnson recalls writing him another fan letter after the composer had given a magnificent performance of the E flat piano quartet of Schumann with the Amadeus. Britten replied that Johnson must have been crazy to like his playing – 'my scrabbled brain and scrabbled fingers'. In fact, he was at his height as a chamber music executant.

While at the Red House, Johnson became increasingly aware that a large project was afoot, although he was not at once told about it. It proved to be *Death in Venice*. (Britten was always careful not to allow any work's genesis to be revealed until the moment was deemed just.) Britten had in mind that Johnson, whom he saw as a budding composer, should prepare the vocal score. It was a kind gesture: Johnson was just leaving the Academy and needing work. For about three weeks, Johnson struggled with the task under the tutelage of Rosamund Strode (q.v.), but it soon became clear that his knowledge of this kind of work was not sufficient, particularly as it had to be completed very quickly. He was proving the weak link in the chain because of lack of experience. Britten wrote him a five-page letter explaining why he would have to be dropped. Somehow Britten managed to put himself in Johnson's position; he knew he would be upset, but he felt it was for the best. 'He remembered what it was like to be a humble beginner. But it was an ill wind that blew nobody any good. He had got out my cello sonata, which I had sent him some time before, and realized that some of the flaws he found in my copying had been evident in the writing of my own work. His advice was invaluable and simple – as, for instance, his insistence that a minim must actually look as if it lasts for four whole quavers, taking up four times the space. At the end he told me to learn by the experience. I wrote back by return that I was sorry I had failed him, but that I would be delighted to act, as he wanted, as a repetiteur. Indeed, I played for all the preparatory sessions when Peter was learning the role of Aschenbach. Had I tried to argue with Ben's decision, or turned the whole thing into an embarrassing episode, I'm certain that I would have lost his friendship. He didn't have the time to smooth damaged egos, and he'd already written me a kind letter.'

After he had finished the opera, and before his operation, Britten worked with Johnson on two of his cycles – the *Hölderlin Fragments* and *Winter Words*. It was immediately apparent what an inspiring teacher he could have been, just how keen was his ear. 'The opening passage of the *Hölderlin* is in double octaves, played forte. He could hear at once that not every octave was sounding in the thumb and the little finger. He insisted that I try it again, making the octaves more even. 'I want to hear the thumb on the B flat and G.' He had, in popular TV parlance, a bionic ear; he could hone in on things that, to less perceptive ears, were just a blur.

'He was also interesting about the pedal, which he used all the time. If it was *not* to be used, his music would be marked to indicate this. His half-pedal playing was extraordinary, but it came from his ear; he couldn't teach it. If you compare the beginning of his record of 'The Foggy Foggy Dew' with that by another pianist, you hear the difference between a mood creator of consummate ability and a good player.'

Graham Johnson's other study with the composer, for *Winter Words*, led to a master class, attended by many well-known musicians, including Walton. 'Sitting in the back row was Ben. I was just about to start when I realized with the utmost relief that he appeared to have gone. His chair was empty. Once the performance was over, he suddenly emerged on stage from nowhere, and said a number of complimentary things followed by a criticism of details. I expressed amazement, wondering how he could have heard the performance. He said that he had stood behind a screen, so as not to put me off my stroke. That was another indication of his empathy with me as a young player. He hadn't lost touch with what it was like to be a beginner.'

All his advice was severely practical. He seldom talked high philosophy, allowing that to take care of itself. This was in stark contrast to Stravinsky, who surrounded himself with writers and poets, people who verbalized about music. Britten could tell a singer where to breathe, or how to phrase, and he would thus make the performance work. How sad that he is not there to pass on that sort of advice at the Maltings school! Of course, he was just that much more responsive, as with Murray Perahia (q.v.) and *Liederkreis*, when he saw there was an artist with the imagination to carry out what he had in mind.

He was also absolutely precise about what he wanted in his music, and Pears never let familiarity breed contempt in executing his friend's wishes. If there were any point of doubt in rehearsing when Britten was not present, he would be referred to by telephone if necessary. It was like being able to consult Schubert, had he been still alive, during the preparation of one of his songs.

In his visits to the Red House, Johnson found conversation veering between musical and domestic matters. 'My enthusiasm to talk about his music must have wearied him. He must have thought of me as something like a *Panorama* interviewer.' They often talked about Stravinsky, whom Britten considered a clever man with notes, but not to much discernible purpose; and about Shostakovich: 'He liked his ability to communicate, and in that respect found in Shostakovich a real soul brother.' He admired Poulenc. That is evidenced by the fact that he did *Mamelles de Tirésias* at Aldeburgh – and took part in the performance. He also performed *Tel jour, telle nuit* with Pears on a number of occasions.

Johnson found him disinclined to talk about his own music. 'He didn't like to be analytical for the purposes of savouring his own triumphs and achievements. It was as if there were something secret and sacred about creative flow that would somehow be spoilt by too much talk or self-conscious analysis. When he left the breakfast table to compose, he went off into a special world. As far as house guests were concerned, he was like Sir Walter Scott, who gave no indication whatsoever what he was writing; indeed, everyone wondered how Scott had so much time to write because he was such a charming host, who gave so much attention to his guests. Britten preferred to talk about the garden, the vegetables, perhaps general artistic matters, rather than talking deeply about himself. He was at the furtherest extreme from a famous singer I once met who, talking of one of his roles, said, "Yes, that *was* one of my finest assumptions."

'Nevertheless, there's no doubt he was a very hard worker; indeed, he once said, "I believe, that a composer is a manual worker, because of the number of notes he gets through." In order for so much music to be written in such a short time, particularly during the late forties and early fifties when he offered an opera a year, he had to devise a very efficient means of operating. That's why everything and everyone about him had to be up to his level of acuteness and efficiency. If he was angry with someone, it was often not a personal matter; it was simply because they had got in the way of this extraordinary work that had to proceed along a pre-ordained timetable. He expected everybody to have the same ultra-professional attitude as he did. In my experience, his demands were understandable when set side by side with what he set himself to achieve.'

Johnson saw Britten for the last time at a concert in the Jubilee Hall a couple of months before his death. 'Peter and I were performing the *Cabaret Songs*, written in the thirties, and a Noel Coward group. I remember Ben sitting in his wheelchair. Even then his presence was such that every performer was put on his mettle. Just having him in the audience was an unforgettable experience.'

28

William Servaes

Servaes, who succeeded Reiss (q.v.) as general manager in 1971, found Britten collected, resourceful and magisterial. There was the constant feeling that he was on a peak and that, for instance, if required he could ring Madam Furtseva (once Russian cultural minister in Moscow) and things would happen. In other words, if he wanted something to be achieved, it would be.

Britten was a great respecter of other people's professional expertise. Servaes likes to work with people who are precise and efficient; it was an attribute he shared with Britten. So in that there was a meeting of minds. Britten also liked people to say what they felt, provided it was to him and that he respected them. He did not like to be pushed around. If he decided a first night was to be on a particular date, that was when it had to be. If that proved impossible for one reason or another, things could become quite torrid for a while.

He was always concerned about what other artists were doing. He would attend as many rehearsals of concerts as possible, even if this made problems for him with his own rehearsals. Anxious that visiting artists should at all times be properly looked after, he was altogether solicitous towards his colleagues and felt himself one of a band of musicians.

There was always a mutual exchange of ideas between Britten and Pears about what should be performed at each festival. Britten was possibly the more practical of the two, and he was always willing to make changes even in his own works to accommodate the existing situation; he was willing at the premiere of *A Midsummer Night's Dream*, for instance, to rewrite the harp part for one instrument as there was space for only one in the Jubilee Hall.

Even the appointment of Servaes as general manager could be cited in evidence of Britten's practicality. Servaes had taken a house at Orford, The Rectory; having just resigned from another post, he was a free agent. Colin Graham (q.v.), who knew him, suggested he might run the festival to which Servaes replied, 'Out of the frying pan, into the fire.' At first he was invited to run the festival as a caretaker manager but, thinking that would not work, he applied for the post, which had then been advertised. But he said that he would not accept it without first having met Britten and Pears. After a performance of *The Turn of the Screw* in 1971, Servaes and his wife received an invitation to the Red House. Immediately he seemed to be in sympathy with Britten. That was the start of their professional relationship.

Because of the difficulties arising from the resignation of Stephen Reiss (q.v.), morale in the festival organization was low and Servaes had a hard few months pulling things together. There was also the question of the money needed to run and develop the Maltings. Servaes, with complete conviction in Britten as an artist, felt that he had to give him whole-hearted backing in what he was trying to achieve at Snape, and went all out to raise funds. At first, the plans were somewhat grandiose (for a large arts centre), but Servaes convinced Britten that they should confine themselves to what they knew about, i.e. music; and they should use only the buildings already leased there. In any case, Britten was not intending to be closely involved in the development of the school and so forth; this was to be left to Pears and Servaes, while he devoted himself more and more to composing.

Servaes never felt he should impose in any way on Britten. He respected his sensitivity as an artist, never calling at the Red House unless summoned. However, in the time of the composer's last illness, they drew closer, and Britten often went to Orford for a meal with Servaes and his wife, and on holiday with them to Venice. In spite of his frequent indisposition, Britten remained buoyant in spirit.

As far as festival programmes were concerned, Servaes always felt that there was an added dimension if Britten was in the audience. Artists would certainly feel that there was a frisson about the occasion; they might feel frightened beforehand, but when it came to the music they gave that little extra to try to please him.

Servaes remembers two telling incidents during the preparation of *Death in Venice*. One afternoon he was sitting in the garden with Britten when the composer said that he had great difficulty that morning in finding a way of 'getting the boat to Venice'. The more he thought about it the larger became the orchestra. Then suddenly he had found the solution – and, with his mouth, hands and knees, he demonstrated it to Servaes, who could graphically hear at that point the ship moving along the Adriatic. It was a keen example to Servaes that, as is well known, Britten felt that the simpler a thing was the better.

A little while afterwards Servaes walked into the library at the Red House one day. Britten appeared to be out of sight; then he suddenly entered, seemingly from nowhere, gave Servaes a score and said, 'There's your opera for next year's festival.' He had just completed it and, childlike, wanted to make that kind of dramatic gesture.

In observing the relationship between Britten and Pears, Servaes saw that the composer was quite riveted by his friend. If Pears had been away singing for some time, Britten could think of nothing else apart from seeing him again. He was always anxious to impart to Pears the latest anecdotes and gossip, always delighting in the relating of small disasters. When they were all in Venice together and the Danieli was flooded, Britten was greatly amused that all the bills were floating about on the water. It was typical of his mischievous humour which emerged if things did not turn out quite right.

Pears was on the whole the better mixer. It was he who would always take the brunt of any public social occasion, whereas Britten stayed in the background. On the other hand, in practical and business matters, Britten was the more decisive and acute. In that respect, as in musical matters, Britten was the thorough professional; but he hated to sweat blood on inessentials.

If, for any reason, an artist did not appear, Britten and Pears were always willing to provide a quickly improvised evening. Britten also liked to do the unusual – as on the occasion in 1972 when he played the two-minute piece, *The Lord of Burghley*, with Deanne Bergsma dancing to it. Britten did realize latterly that this impromptu quality had rather gone out of the festival. He was no longer to be found turning the pages for the likes of Fischer-Dieskau. It was inevitable, certainly once the Maltings was in existence, that the festival had a more formal structure. He appreciated the gains and losses.

Servaes sometimes felt uneasy working for Britten simply because the composer was such a special person; but that also helped to make their working relationship fascinating. There were occasions when the atmosphere could be cut with a knife when something did not work out as he wished. One such was the première of *Death in Venice*, when Colin Graham, from London, had asked for the date to be postponed. It was early days for Servaes at the festival and in all innocence he conveyed this fact to Britten. The result was as if a bolt of lightning had struck. Britten was so incensed that he said that he thought the whole project was put into question. The fracas went on for five days, while Servaes negotiated with Keith Grant (q.v.) and Graham (q.v.). Eventually, of course, Britten got his way, and Graham's other commitments, which caused the clash, were altered accordingly. That kind of incident did not occur frequently, perhaps because Servaes learnt quickly that Britten had one skin less than anyone else, and had to be treated accordingly.

Servaes is anxious to emphasize that, as with everyone, Britten had varying sides to his character. 'He was not always the saintly person portrayed in the film *A Time There Was*, nor was he simply petulant. He had charm, perfect manners, concern for friends and their kin, but he could be obstinate and forceful when the occasion arose. Whatever the faults, they were forgotten in the light of the artist's undoubted greatness.'

29

Murray Perahia

Murray Perahia got to know Britten shortly after he had won the Leeds International Piano Competition in 1972, when they were introduced by Marion Thorpe. Prior to that, however, he had attended every concert Britten and Peter Pears had ever given in New York. There were two accounts of *Winterreise*, and at least one of *Dichterliebe*, at the end of which many of the audience were weeping. What Perahia gleaned from these recitals was a certain kind of intimate rapport that he had never heard before in music. The performances were indelibly stamped with the imprint of Britten and Pears, yet at the same time there was an evident obedience and reverence for the composer's wishes. It was a moving experience.

After Leeds, Mrs Thorpe asked Perahia if he would like to come to her house at Aldeburgh, where there was to be a recital by Pears and Britten of English song. He delayed his return to the US to make the journey to Suffolk. It was to be Britten's last appearance on the recital platform. Again, Perahia was stirred by the singing and playing. Here at Aldeburgh the atmosphere he had found so arresting in New York was more or less taken for granted; what struck him now was the extraordinary sound Britten brought out of the piano. The musical control was incredible, in the sense that he managed to make every song into a single statement. Afterwards, Perahia met the composer for the first time and was greeted by an apology from Britten for his playing – he said he had not touched the piano for some time before the concert. That amazed Perahia, who had been spellbound by the playing.

Britten also said that he would like to play four hands with a real pianist. Lunch next day was a little embarrassing in that Britten spent some time attacking competitions. Although Perahia agreed with the composer's views, he could hardly appear at that point to do so.

The following year in the autumn, at the Edinburgh Festival, Pears (who was singing in *Death in Venice*) was staying at the same hotel as Perahia, who decided to ask him whether they might have breakfast together. Pears had attended Perahia's concerto performance the previous night. At breakfast, Pears asked him if, as Britten was no longer able to play with him, he would like to accompany him at the following year's Aldeburgh Festival (1974). Perahia practically dropped his teacup with surprise and immediately agreed to the suggestion. A Schumann programme was arranged. When the time came for the festival, Perahia was overwhelmed to find Britten attending the rehearsal for the recital. He had already worked with Pears in London, so they were well prepared but, after the Aldeburgh rehearsal, Britten was anxious to go through almost every song of the *Liederkreis* on which he had made notes. All the comments focused on the main weaknesses and difficulties of what he had just heard. This hour of coaching touched only on essentials. He advised on how to begin a song (by establishing through rhythmic and tonal emphasis), how to end it (by distilling the essential mood and reflecting it), how to approach the bass line so as to help the singer to project more easily, and many other subtleties in the art of accompanying. He also said that every great piece had some specific emotion to impart, and it was the artist's duty to find that.

Perahia found himself, not unnaturally, very nervous for the recital in the afternoon. He tried to carry out as much as possible of what he had been told. At the party at the Red House afterwards, Britten expressed thanks for what had been achieved but said that he would like to work further with Perahia, who himself took him the *Hölderlin* settings, which he was preparing with Pears.

That proved, as Perahia puts it, 'one of the most moving moments of my musical life' because, although Britten was partially paralysed in his right hand, he was able to show

Perahia how he wanted the triplet figure in the second song to sound: the composer wanted it to appear as though it had no beginning or end, and so he suggested that it should be played as a pulsation without accents. Perahia was unable quite to achieve the effect. So Britten went to the piano himself. In spite of his impediment, he played right through the piece; it was amazingly beautiful. It proved that he hardly needed to practise – that much of his inspiration at the piano was conceived in his mind. He recalls that the bass was brought out yet remained part of the texture. Also, the shaping of the song to its inevitable climax was just right. It was also a touching experience as this was the first (and perhaps only) time that Pears and Britten performed a song together after his operation.

On another occasion, Perahia went through the Pushkin cycle, *The Poet's Echo*, with the composer. Britten played a little of the last song, where he so evocatively represents the clock ticking, and once more the example to Perahia was extraordinary; had he not heard Britten playing, he would not have been able to fulfil the cycle's precise requirements. Britten's advice in some of the other songs was so vivid that Perahia found himself able afterwards to reach to their heart, particularly in the matter of capturing the needed rhythmic intensity.

Later, Perahia took him the Schumann concerto – to the cottage at Horham, where Britten spent many of his later days. Perahia was astonished to find that, before he arrived, Britten had taken the trouble to study closely the first movement. After he had heard Perahia play through it once, they discussed at some length the clash of E and F major chords stated at the very beginning of the concerto and worked out in the cadenza. (Britten's approach was not intellectual, but basically a study through melody. Indeed structural analysis was not for him; he told Perahia to study music through Schubert, with melody uppermost in the mind. Melody must always be in a player's thoughts as he prepared a work in his mind or at the keyboard.)

On this day, they went through the whole of the Schumann. When Perahia played it for a radio broadcast, he received a card from Britten encouraging him but suggesting a more relaxed attitude. The following summer, after Perahia had again played the concerto, this time at Aldeburgh, Britten made specific criticisms. He wanted the work's first theme taken faster – at a real Allegro – not drawn out as it usually is. He also wanted the syncopated theme in the finale accentuated quite differently. He felt that the cello theme in the slow movement should not be sentimentalized. All these ideas seemed right to Perahia, even if he feels that he has never quite brought them off in a performance. Perahia was very appreciative that Britten's musical conscience insisted on his making these criticisms and suggestions. It showed, too, that the cliché-ridden reading was anathema to the composer.

There were a few other occasions when insights were imparted: Britten pointed out a mistaken rhythm in the last of Schumann's *Fantasiestücke* (a point never made by any teacher), further work on Britten's songs, and suggested a way to play the accompaniment of Schumann's 'Mein Wagen rollet langsam' to give that curious song a hypnotic effect, the dignity needed in accompanying Haydn's 'She never told her love'. But Perahia was reluctant to take him any more large-scale works for fear of tiring the composer. A piano piece suggested for Perahia sadly was not to be.

Britten was always trying to influence Perahia's programmes to exclude Beethoven. There were fairly acid comments about Op.110, which Britten had had to play as a boy. They sometimes upset Perahia. When Britten realized this, he told Perahia of an occasion in Australia when he had made similar criticisms and been chastised by a student for destroying an idol. He felt after that that he should keep to himself many of his views about Beethoven – and Brahms. Perahia thinks that Britten found Beethoven too intellectual, in the sense that his melodies had often been worked out in great detail and did not flow as naturally as Schubert's, for example. They were not vocal tunes. He was also chary of the insistence in Beethoven's musical make-up. Perahia did not agree with this prejudice of Britten's but he is well aware that a composer has to have that kind of strong opinion if he is to have a personality of his own. It is natural that, for instance, Tchaikovsky should not have liked Bach.

Voice always played the most important part in Britten's musical thought and conversation. He told Perahia that he considered counterpoint as the most important aspect of composition to study, because of the need to learn to hear two voices, one against the other. That's what makes harmony; if you think of harmony as an entity in itself, it becomes too structural and you are not aware of the voices interrelating. Perahia also responded to that kind of musical thinking.

When they discussed Brahms, Perahia found that Britten quite admired that composer's earlier works. He liked the first movement of the D minor concerto, disliked the B flat. He liked the passion and spontaneity in the former; elsewhere he did not find much spontaneity in Brahms. Britten seemed to think that the best Brahms was composed before Schumann, whom he so much loved, died. After that something went out of him.

Schubert, of course, was Britten's greatest idol. He always found it incredible that Schubert was thinking of going to study with someone the year before he died. Britten would laugh, wondering what that teacher would say to Schubert who had just composed the C major quintet. Maybe: 'I don't think the voice leading is good enough'!

He did not respond to Schoenberg, and that was not for want of trying. When the music was published, he had learnt Op.11, and later in his library Perahia found the score with all Britten's fingerings. Before that, when his school library refused to stock *Pierrot Lunaire* because it was too modern, Britten went elsewhere to obtain the score so that he could study it. He felt that the music was too intellectual, insufficiently beautiful. Of that school, as is known, he liked only Berg. He was just as industrious in earlier days in studying Stravinsky. He liked to hear Stravinsky's work, but was not sure how much of it, apart from the first great outpourings, would stand the test of time.

Although he had an appreciation of – and often performed – many songs by British composers of the twentieth century with Pears, they both felt that very often these songs failed to depict the emotional atmosphere of a poem; the texts became 'churchified'. Perhaps that explains why the *Michelangelo Sonnets*, when they first appeared, made such an impression, they tangled with the hidden aspects of the words. The piano part really delved deep into the meaning of the poems, rather than just adding harmony to the vocal line.

Stimulated by a meeting on a Jewish holy day, the two discussed religious beliefs. Perahia asked the composer if he thought of himself as religious. Britten replied that he was certainly a Christian in his music. Although he could not accept church doctrine, he believed in a God and a destiny.

Perahia was very aware of Britten's generosity, particularly towards young people. On one occasion, for instance, Britten discovered a trouble-maker in a school choir and went to talk to him. He discovered the boy had an unsatisfactory home life, and no money; so he decided to pay for part of the boy's education. 'The compassion that is to be felt in the music was also there in the man.'

30

Colin Matthews

Working Notes

Although Britten's illness subsequent to his heart operation in the spring of 1973 caused him considerable difficulties in composing and writing out his music (his right side had been affected by a slight stroke), it was not until the composition of *Phaedra* in the summer of 1975 that he felt the need of direct assistance. Playing through work-in-progress on the piano had always been, for Britten, an important part of the composing process. Because the weakness of his right hand prevented him from doing this adequately, he asked me if I would play through *Phaedra* as he composed it, an experiment which was successful enough for the same procedure to be followed with the third string quartet. The *Welcome Ode*, a much simpler score, needed a different approach.

Phaedra: Summer 1975

There were two sessions, both at Aldeburgh, on 7 and 27 August. On 4 August I discussed with Ben in the garden of the Red House (it was an extremely hot day) the problems involved, and I took away a photocopy of the first seven pages of full score, up to Figure 5. (Britten composed *Phaedra* in full score – unusually for him – having first marked his copy of Lowell's text as well as making a few brief sketches.) Before the first session took place, I had received copies of a further thirteen pages, as far as Figure 18. Britten had, by 7 August, composed some way beyond this point – at least as far as Figure 23.

The main problem for me at the first session (we worked in the Red House library) was to make an adequate account of the full score at the piano – I had not had time to make a piano reduction. Particularly difficult was the string figuration following figure 9, and the approximation which appears in the vocal score was what I worked out to Ben's satisfaction at this session. He himself sat beside me at the right-hand end of the keyboard, and generally played the vocal line with his left hand.

The following is a list of those things which stood out as needing particular attention (references are to the published vocal score):

In the first bars Ben was especially anxious to hear the string chord sustained from the opening melody.

Figure 3:
Some of the recitative was tried out on the harpsichord (see also second session).

Figure 5:
Throughout the Presto Ben wanted the timpani emphasized – he wanted to hear a very percussive sound. (NB it was never satisfactorily established how the timpani were to be played. At first Britten wrote 'ruthe – brush', i.e. with switches but, since this was not satisfactory to his ears in rehearsal, side drumsticks were used at the first performance instead. On the recording – made after Britten's death – side drumsticks near the rim seemed to produce the right sort of sound, but the question must remain open. In the coda, wire brushes are probably the answer.)

Figure 8:
This passage was originally marked 'gracefully'. Ben here played the vocal line forcefully in octaves with his left hand.

Figure 9:
Ben asked me to play through the bar before and the first bar of Figure 9 slowly and carefully several times. He made no changes, but was anxious to hear the harmonic movement as

clearly as possible. From the sixth bar of Figure 9 Ben wanted the F in the bass emphasized. The four bars before Figure 10 were also played through very slowly, the movement of the bass being particularly important.

The two bars before Figure 13 were, again, played through slowly, and the E in the following bars emphasized.

The first bar of the cello solo beginning six bars before Figure 14 went through three stages, the point seeming to be how clearly A major should be established:

In order to clarify this, I played through the previous two bars as well many times.

The third bar before Figure 14 was played through several times slowly.

Immediately after this first session I started making the piano reduction. The rest of the full score arrived about a week later (Britten completed *Phaedra* on 12 August), and by the second session on 27 August I was able to play the complete work in vocal score. This meant that there were far fewer problems:

At Figure 18 the harpsichord was again used to test the effect of playing on two manuals.

From Figure 21 onwards the important rhythm 𝅗𝅥. ♩ ♩ ♩ in the Ms was changed throughout to ♩ 𝅗𝅥 𝅗𝅥 ♩. Ben had not *quite* made up his mind that this was what he wanted.

The harmony from Figure 22 was played through slowly, and the transition at Figure 23 played several times.

Ben's main concern was with the ending – the transition to Figure 29. After a lot of thought and numerous playthroughs, he decided to reject the extended version (see music example A at end) because it 'held up the action'. Although he didn't want to lose the music, he felt that the sudden cut-off after Phaedra's last words was more effective.

A few minor changes were made later to the vocal score. The full score was copied by Rosamund Strode.

String Quartet No.3: Autumn–Winter 1975

There were three sessions on the quartet: 22 and 23 October, 8 December and 17 December.

I saw the work for the first time on the morning of 22 October, and played through to Ben the first movement in detail, and most of the second movement in the afternoon. At that time he had composed as far as bar 102 of the second movement: in fact there were only four more bars. On the afternoon of 23 October, most of the time was spent on the second movement, which had only been looked at briefly the previous day.

The following were the most important points:

First movement
Bar 14 ff: The pizzicatos were brought out; pedal points were of particular importance (cf. bars 58 ff.).

Bar 18: In this and similar bars, Ben wanted the viola 'flourish' played carefully – he made it clear that it was melodic and not just colouristic.

Bar 36: the viola's C natural was to be emphasized.

Bar 40 ff.: The whole of the 3/4 section was played very slowly and carefully with emphasis on the harmonic movement.

Bar 57: This bar was a later insertion: the music originally went straight from bar 56 to bar 58.

Bar 58 ff.: This passage, especially bars 60 to 63, caused more problems than any other. The first cello note in bar 61 was originally C above middle C, changed to E above that, before it became G; while the cello C in bar 62 was at first the F a fourth higher. The single notes were crucial to this passage, and had to be played many times until Ben was satisfied that they were the right ones.

Bars 64 to 75: Ben originally considered cutting these twelve bars, on the grounds that the movement was too long. On the photocopy of the manuscript with which I worked I notated down the following bar of music, which was intended as the link between bar 63 and bar 76:

Ben was, however, rather reluctant to make this cut and, when the finale proved to be much longer than he had expected, he was ready, without much prompting, to restore the passage so that the first movement would 'balance' the finale.

Second Movement

The difficulty of playing this movement at anything like the proper tempo was considerable. As far as possible, Ben played the ostinato – at various pitches – with his left hand.

Bar 1 ff.: The harmony of the opening bars was played through several times very slowly.

Bar 38 ff.: The harmony and the interweaving of parts here was very important. Bar 47 (which was originally in 3/4) was played many times, together with bar 46.

Bar 49 ff.: The harmony of the moving parts still important, especially bars 58 to 61. (Ben had some difficulty with playing the ostinato here.)

Britten completed the first four movements of the quartet by the end of October, and in November went for a holiday to Venice, where he composed the Finale. I received photocopies of the third and fourth movements shortly before the second session, but did not see the finale until I was in Aldeburgh on 8 December.

Third movement
There were no problems in playing this through – except that I failed to notice the key change from F to A flat in bar 42 – which Ben was amused to point out. In the final bars he had written a few alternatives to the solo violin, with a view to making the line less diatonic; but he didn't in fact ask me to play the alternatives as he was (quite rightly!) very satisfied with it as it was.

Fourth movement
This was again very difficult to play. There were no real problems, but the fugato from bar 37 was virtually impossible for me to play two-handed, and it was difficult for Ben to fit an extra part in. I played it very slowly (and badly). In the Trio, Ben played the first violin part. The transition back – bars 97 to 106 – was played through several times, but no changes were made.

Finale
Bar 1: Ben had forgotton to put 'pizz.' against the viola – which was immediately apparent from the way in which I played it. Throughout the introduction, he was very insistent that I got the tempi right. (All the metronome marks in the published score are mine, established while playing the work through.) It was clear that Ben didn't want the recitatives played too freely.

Bars 13 to 15: The harmony here, and more importantly in bars 17 and 18, was played slowly and carefully, as it also was in bars 20 to 22. As far as I remember, I first played through the introduction piecemeal, stopping every now and then, and then as a whole.

Bar 26: Ben considered adding a pause on the first beat of the bar.

Throughout the passacaglia, Ben played the cello part – the only time in any session that he had played the bass. There were no problems: I had made a piano reduction of some of the three-part writing (from bar 50) in order to facilitate reading – Ben wanted to hear some of this twice. I played the ending several times (but *not* the crossed out original ending, see example B). Of the final chord, Ben said to me, 'I want the work to end with a question.'

The third session, 17 December, took place at my suggestion that my brother David and I should play through the whole work four-handed. Ben was very agreeable to this, although rather nervous at the idea of a 'performance'. At this stage, the definitive transition in the first movement between bars 57 and 58 had been established, as well as the expansion of the original two final bars of the movement into three. Neither of these changes had been played before.

Paradoxically, the first movement proved initially more difficult with four hands than it had with two (or three), and the problems caused Ben to become rather agitated. The fourth movement, however, was found to work very well.

After lunch, and some rehearsal, we played through the whole quartet, which pleased Ben greatly. There was some light-hearted discussion about whether the quartet might not be too long to fit on an LP side – the work had proved to be quite a bit longer than he had anticipated – and Ben was in a relaxed and benevolent mood.

The score was copied out by Rosamund Strode; in October 1976 the Amadeus Quartet played through the work for Britten in the Red House library – the only time he was to hear it. I should add that, initially, Britten referred to the work as a 'Divertimento'. It was typical of his unassuming nature that he didn't think it was 'serious' enough to be given the title of String Quartet.

Welcome Ode: Summer 1976

Because of the relative simplicity of Britten's last completed work, there was no necessity to play it through on the piano. But his increasing weakness (especially in the extreme heat of that summer) made him very reluctant to attempt to write out a full score. So it was agreed that I should prepare the score from Britten's sketches, and show it to him at every stage. While the

EX. A

EX. B

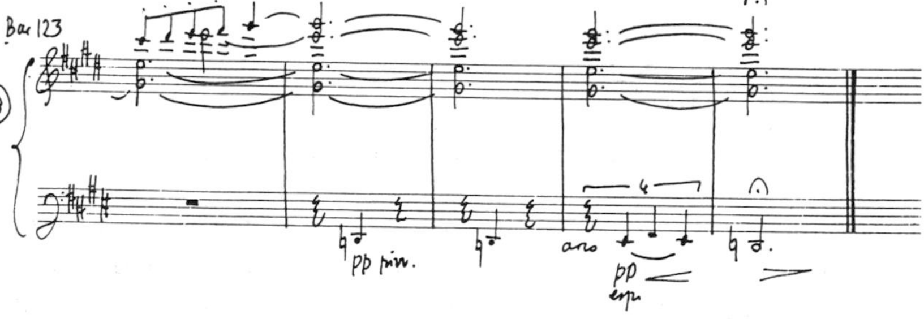

overall responsibility for the scoring was to be mine (a rather alarming prospect), Britten would supervise it throughout; and he made many changes and suggestions to the score as it progressed. (A microfilm of all the pages of the full score that contain Britten's additions is in the Britten–Pears Library.) We talked a little about this project in June during the rehearsals for the first performance of *Phaedra*; and, at the end of July, Rosamund Strode and I visited a summer school at which the Suffolk Schools Orchestra was playing. Our report on this led Ben to suggest, at our first proper session at Horham, on 29 July, that it might be best to make a very simplified score, using only 'high register', 'middle register' instruments, etc. But he agreed that this might make the players feel that they were being written down to, and so the scoring was established as standard orchestra with as many *ad lib* instruments as possible.

I began the score working from Ben's sketch (which had very few indications of instrumentation), and sending sections to him as they were finished. (At this time the work was called simply *Cantata*.) The composition of the piece was finished on 19 August, and our next session was at Horham on the 24th. On 8 September we had a third session, at Aldeburgh, and on 20 September I completed the draft orchestration and sent the whole score to Ben. By this time the orchestration of the first three sections was more or less established, and our last session, on 8 October completed the work to Britten's satisfaction. We arranged our next meeting for 9 November, to start work in the same way on the cantata *Praise We Great Men*, but this had to be cancelled at the very last moment; I was not to see Ben again.